USA Trivia Quiz Book:

American History, Geography and Culture

*Thank you to Michael Griffin and his friends for playing trivia in the basement instead of what I thought you were really doing. This was made for you and your fantastic friends

Table of Contents

Chapter 1	The United States Constitution...pg 1
Chapter 2	The Presidents of the United States of America...pg 16
Chapter 3	The First Ladies of the United States...pg 31
Chapter 4	The 50 States...pg 48
Chapter 5	U.S. Geography...pg 63
Chapter 6	The American Revolutionary War...pg 78
Chapter 7	American Inventors...pg 94
Chapter 8	American Athletics...pg 109
Chapter 9	Do You Know the State Capitals? pg 125
Chapter 10	Fun Facts About Our State Capitals...pg 140
Chapter 11	Legendary American Sporting Events...pg 157
Chapter 12	American Television...pg 173
Chapter 13	America's National Parks, Rivers & Lakes...pg 189
Chapter 14	America's Mountains and Mountain Ranges...pg 205

*Answers are at the end of each chapter

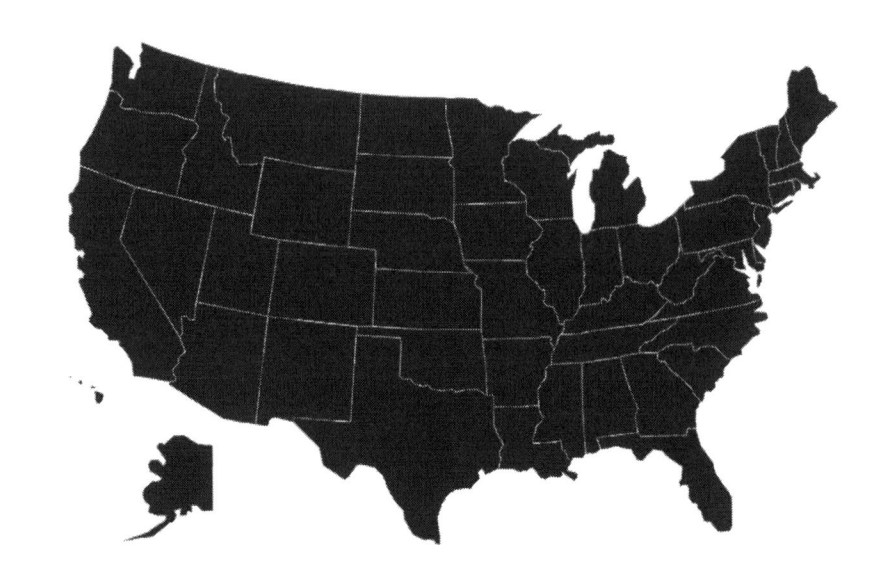

Chapter 1

The United States Constitution

1. What year was the United States Constitution signed?

a) 1776

b) 1781

c) 1787

d) 1791

2. Which of the following is known as the "Supreme Law of the Land"?

a) The Declaration of Independence

b) The Articles of Confederation

c) The U.S. Constitution

d) The Bill of Rights

3. How many amendments does the U.S. Constitution currently have?

a) 10

b) 27

c) 33

d) 45

4. What is the main purpose of the Preamble of the Constitution?

a) To establish the legislative branch

b) To introduce the Constitution's goals and purposes

c) To outline the rights of the states

d) To set up the system of checks and balances

5. Which branch of government is established in Article I of the Constitution?

a) Executive

b) Legislative

c) Judicial

d) Administrative

6. Who is considered the "Father of the Constitution"?

a) George Washington

b) Thomas Jefferson

c) James Madison

d) Benjamin Franklin

7. Which body has the power to impeach the President?

a) The Senate

b) The House of Representatives

c) The Supreme Court

d) The Electoral College

8. What fraction of states is required to ratify an amendment to the Constitution?

a) 1/2

b) 2/3

c) 3/4

d) 4/5

9. Which amendment guarantees freedom of speech?

a) 1st

b) 2nd

c) 3rd

d) 4th

10. How long is the term of a U.S. Senator?

a) 2 years

b) 4 years

c) 6 years

d) 8 years

11. Which amendment abolished slavery in the United States?

a) 13th

b) 14th

c) 15th

d) 19th

12. Which branch of government is responsible for interpreting the Constitution?

a) Executive

b) Legislative

c) Judicial

d) Electoral

13. The system of checks and balances is designed to do what?

a) Ensure all branches of government have equal power

b) Allow the President to have more power

c) Strengthen the legislative branch

d) Allow states to nullify federal laws

14. Only two signers of the Constitution later became president. Name the two.

a) Alexander Hamilton and John Adams

b) Thomas Jefferson and James Madison

c) George Washington and James Madison

d) Benjamin Franklin and George Washington

15. The 19th Amendment to the Constitution granted which group the right to vote?

a) African Americans

b) Women

c) Immigrants

d) Native Americans

16. What is the minimum age for a U.S. Representative?

a) 25

b) 30

c) 35

d) 40

17. Which case established the principle of judicial review?

a) Brown v. Board of Education

b) Marbury v. Madison

c) Plessy v. Ferguson

d) Roe v. Wade

18. How many justices are on the Supreme Court?

a) 7

b) 9

c) 11

d) 13

19. Which amendment limits the President to two terms?

a) 20th

b) 22nd

c) 24th

d) 25th

20. The Fifth Amendment protects against what?

a) Cruel and unusual punishment

b) Self-incrimination

c) Double jeopardy

d) b and c

21. Who presides over the Senate when the Vice President is absent?

a) The Speaker of the House

b) The Majority Leader

c) The President pro tempore

d) The Chief Justice

22. Which branch of government has the power to declare war?

a) Executive

b) Legislative

c) Judicial

d) Administrative

23. The 8th Amendment protects against what?

a) Double jeopardy

b) Cruel and unusual punishment

c) Self-incrimination

d) Unreasonable searches and seizures

24. How many states had to ratify the Constitution for it to become effective?

a) 7

b) 9

c) 11

d) 13

25. The 14th Amendment addresses which issue?

a) Women's suffrage

b) Equal protection under the law

c) Prohibition

d) Income tax

26. The original purpose of the Constitutional Convention was to:

a) Draft the U.S. Constitution

b) Amend the Articles of Confederation

c) Elect the first President

d) Establish a federal judiciary

27. Which part of the Constitution outlines the powers of the President?

a) Article I

b) Article II

c) Article III

d) Article IV

28. The 2nd Amendment deals with the right to:

a) Free speech

b) Bear arms

c) A fair trial

d) Vote

29. Who was the first President to be impeached?

a) Andrew Jackson

b) Andrew Johnson

c) Richard Nixon

d) Bill Clinton

30. What does the term "bicameral" refer to?

a) Two houses of Congress

b) Two political parties

c) Two terms of the President

d) Two branches of government

31. The necessary and proper clause is also known as:

a) The Supremacy Clause

b) The Elastic Clause

c) The Commerce Clause

d) The Equal Protection Clause

32. Which amendment gave 18-year-olds the right to vote?

a) 23rd

b) 24th

c) 25th

d) 26th

33. What is the main function of the Electoral College?

a) To elect the President and Vice President

b) To pass federal laws

c) To appoint Supreme Court justices

d) To advise the President

34. Which of the following best describes federalism?

a) A single central government

b) A system of government where power is divided between national and state governments

c) A system of checks and balances

d) A parliamentary system

35. What is required to override a presidential veto?

a) A simple majority in both houses of Congress

b) A two-thirds majority in both houses of Congress

c) A unanimous vote in the Senate

d) Approval by the Supreme Court

36. Which was the first state to ratify the Constitution, and which was the last state to ratify, in that order?

a) Virginia and New Jersey

b) Rhode Island and Pennsylvania

c) Delaware and Rhode Island

d) Delaware and New Hampshire

37. "Constitution Day", the anniversary of the signing of the Constitution, is celebrated on what day?

a) November 25

b) July 4

c) September 17

d) February 22

38. Which of the following is NOT a power of Congress under the Constitution?

a) To coin money

b) To declare war

c) To appoint Supreme Court justices

d) To regulate commerce

39. The principle that no one, including government officials, is above the law is known as:

a) Rule of Law

b) Judicial Review

c) Federalism

d) Separation of Powers

40. What word does *not* appear in the U.S. Constitution?

a) Democracy

b) Union

c) Defense

d) Tranquility

41. The 16th Amendment allowed for what?

a) The prohibition of alcohol

b) The direct election of senators

c) The federal income tax

d) Women's suffrage

42. Who has the power to negotiate treaties under the Constitution?

a) The Senate

b) The President

c) The Secretary of State

d) The House of Representatives

43. Which amendment addresses the rights of states and the people?

a) 8th

b) 9th

c) 10th

d) 11th

44. The 4th Amendment protects against:

a) Cruel and unusual punishment

b) Unreasonable searches and seizures

c) Double jeopardy

d) Self-incrimination

45. The "Full Faith and Credit Clause" requires states to:

a) Honor the public acts, records, and judicial proceedings of other states

b) Provide for the common defense

c) Uphold the Constitution

d) Protect civil rights

46. How many branches of government does the Constitution establish?

a) 1

b) 2

c) 3

d) 4

47. The principle of "separation of powers" refers to:

a) Division of powers between the national and state governments

b) Division of government into three branches

c) Division of power between the President and Congress

d) Division of powers within Congress

48. The President must be at least how old to be elected?

a) 30

b) 35

c) 40

d) 45

49. Which of the following best describes the Bill of Rights?

a) The first 10 amendments to the Constitution

b) The Preamble to the Constitution

c) The articles of the Constitution

d) The Federalist Papers

50. Who is responsible for appointing justices to the Supreme Court?

a) The Senate

b) The President

c) The House of Representatives

d) The Chief Justice of the Supreme Court

Answers:

1. c) 1787

2. c) The U.S. Constitution

3. b) 27

4. b) To introduce the Constitution's goals and purposes

5. b) Legislative

6. c) James Madison

7. b) The House of Representatives

8. c) 3/4

9. a) 1st

10. c) 6 years

11. a) 13th

12. c) Judicial

13. a) Ensure all branches of government have equal power

14. c) George Washington and James Madison

15. b) Women

16. a) 25

17. b) Marbury v. Madison

18. b) 9

19. b) 22nd

20. d) b and c

21. c) The President pro tempore

22. b) Legislative

23. b) Cruel and unusual punishment

24. b) 9

25. b) Equal protection under the law

26. b) Amend the Articles of Confederation

27. b) Article II

28. b) Bear arms

29. b) Andrew Johnson

30. a) Two houses of Congress

31. b) The Elastic Clause

32. d) 26th

33. a) To elect the President and Vice President

34. b) A system of government where power is divided between national and state governments

35. b) A two-thirds majority in both houses of Congress

36. c) Delaware and Rhode Island

37. c) September 17

38. c) To appoint Supreme Court justices

39. a) Rule of Law

40. a) Democracy

41. c) The federal income tax

42. b) The President

43. c) 10th

44. b) Unreasonable searches and seizures

45. a) Honor the public acts, records, and judicial proceedings of other states

46. c) 3

47. b) Division of government into three branches

48. b) 35

49. a) The first 10 amendments to the Constitution

50. b) The President

Chapter 2

The Presidents of the United States of America

1. Which President is known for delivering the Gettysburg Address?

a) Ulysses S. Grant

b) Abraham Lincoln

c) Franklin Pierce

d) Andrew Johnson

2. Who was the first President to live in the White House?

a) George Washington

b) John Adams

c) Thomas Jefferson

d) James Madison

3. Which President purchased the Louisiana Territory from France?

a) James Monroe

b) John Quincy Adams

c) Thomas Jefferson

d) James Madison

4. Which U.S. President was a former Hollywood actor?

a) Ronald Reagan

b) George H.W. Bush

c) John F. Kennedy

d) Richard Nixon

5. Who was the youngest person to become President?

a) John F. Kennedy

b) Theodore Roosevelt

c) Bill Clinton

d) Barack Obama

6. Which President was in office during the Cuban Missile Crisis?

a) Dwight D. Eisenhower

b) John F. Kennedy

c) Lyndon B. Johnson

d) Richard Nixon

7. Who was the first President to be impeached twice?

a) Andrew Jackson

b) Donald Trump

c) Richard Nixon

d) Bill Clinton

8. Which President is credited with the New Deal programs?

a) Herbert Hoover

b) Franklin D. Roosevelt

c) Harry S. Truman

d) Dwight D. Eisenhower

9. Who was the only U.S. President to resign from office?

a) Richard Nixon

b) Gerald Ford

c) Jimmy Carter

d) Ronald Reagan

10. Which President was known for the "Square Deal" domestic program?

a) Theodore Roosevelt

b) Woodrow Wilson

c) Calvin Coolidge

d) Herbert Hoover

11. Who was President during the U.S. Civil War?

a) James Buchanan

b) Ulysses S. Grant

c) Abraham Lincoln

d) Andrew Johnson

12. Which President was assassinated in Dallas, Texas in 1963?

a) Harry S. Truman

b) Dwight D. Eisenhower

c) John F. Kennedy

d) Lyndon B. Johnson

13. Who was the first President to appear on television?

a) Franklin D. Roosevelt

b) Harry S. Truman

c) Dwight D. Eisenhower

d) John F. Kennedy

14. Which President signed the Civil Rights Act of 1964 into law?

a) John F. Kennedy

b) Lyndon B. Johnson

c) Richard Nixon

d) Gerald Ford

15. Who was the only President to serve two non-consecutive terms?

a) Grover Cleveland

b) William McKinley

c) Woodrow Wilson

d) Calvin Coolidge

16. Which U.S. President was a general in the Mexican-American War?

a) James Polk

b) Zachary Taylor

c) Millard Fillmore

d) Franklin Pierce

17. Which President's face is carved into Mount Rushmore alongside Washington, Jefferson, and Lincoln?

a) Andrew Jackson

b) Ulysses S. Grant

c) Theodore Roosevelt

d) Woodrow Wilson

18. Who was the first President to win a Nobel Peace Prize?

a) Woodrow Wilson

b) Theodore Roosevelt

c) Jimmy Carter

d) Barack Obama

19. Which U.S. President was known as "Old Hickory"?

a) Andrew Jackson

b) Martin Van Buren

c) William Henry Harrison

d) John Tyler

20. Who was President during the signing of the Camp David Accords in 1978?

a) Richard Nixon

b) Gerald Ford

c) Jimmy Carter

d) Ronald Reagan

21. Which President gave the famous speech that included "Ask not what your country can do for you – ask what you can do for your country"?

a) Franklin D. Roosevelt

b) John F. Kennedy

c) Lyndon B. Johnson

d) Ronald Reagan

22. Which U.S. President signed the Patriot Act into law?

a) Bill Clinton

b) George W. Bush

c) Barack Obama

d) Donald Trump

23. Which President initiated the Lewis and Clark expedition?

a) George Washington

b) John Adams

c) Thomas Jefferson

d) James Madison

24. Which President was in office during the 9/11 attacks?

a) George H.W. Bush

b) Bill Clinton

c) George W. Bush

d) Barack Obama

25. Who was the first U.S. President to be awarded the Congressional Gold Medal?

a) George Washington

b) Thomas Jefferson

c) Abraham Lincoln

d) James Madison

26. Which President issued the famous "Fourteen Points" during World War I?

a) William Howard Taft

b) Woodrow Wilson

c) Warren G. Harding

d) Calvin Coolidge

27. Who was the last U.S. President to be a founding father?

a) Thomas Jefferson

b) James Madison

c) James Monroe

d) John Quincy Adams

28. Which President established the Environmental Protection Agency (EPA)?

a) Lyndon B. Johnson

b) Richard Nixon

c) Gerald Ford

d) Jimmy Carter

29. Who was the first President to be born in a hospital in Plains, Georgia?

a) John F. Kennedy

b) Lyndon B. Johnson

c) Jimmy Carter

d) Ronald Reagan

30. Which U.S. President famously declared, "I am not a crook"?

a) Richard Nixon

b) Gerald Ford

c) Jimmy Carter

d) Ronald Reagan

31. Which President signed the North American Free Trade Agreement (NAFTA)?

a) George H.W. Bush

b) Bill Clinton

c) George W. Bush

d) Barack Obama

32. Who was the oldest person to assume the U.S. Presidency?

a) Donald Trump

b) Ronald Reagan

c) Joe Biden

d) George H.W. Bush

33. Which President delivered the famous "Berlin Wall" speech urging, "Mr. Gorbachev, tear down this wall"?

a) Jimmy Carter

b) Ronald Reagan

c) George H.W. Bush

d) Bill Clinton

34. Who was the first U.S. President to die in office?

a) William Henry Harrison

b) Zachary Taylor

c) Abraham Lincoln

d) James Garfield

35. Which U.S. President served as the head of the CIA before becoming President?

a) Lyndon B. Johnson

b) Richard Nixon

c) George H.W. Bush

d) Gerald Ford

36. Who was the U.S. President to have a dog named "Millie"?

a) George H.W. Bush

b) Bill Clinton

c) Donald Trump

d) Richard Nixon

37. Which U.S. President was a former peanut farmer?

a) Gerald Ford

b) Jimmy Carter

c) Ronald Reagan

d) George H.W. Bush

38. This U.S. President witnessed Abraham Lincoln's funeral procession as a child, in New York City in 1865 and reputedly had a photographic memory.

a) Thomas Jefferson

b) Andrew Jackson

c) Martin Van Buren

d) Theodore Roosevelt

39. Who was the first Catholic President of the United States?

a) Franklin D. Roosevelt

b) John F. Kennedy

c) Lyndon B. Johnson

d) Jimmy Carter

40. Which president suffered a fatal stroke on the floor of the House Chamber?

a) John Quincy Adams

b) Woodrow Wilson

c) Franklin D. Roosevelt

d) William Howard Taft

41. Who was the tallest US president at 6 feet 4 inches and who was the shortest at 5 feet 4 inches, in that order?

a) Andrew Jackson and Richard Nixon

b) Barack Obama and Joe Biden

c) Abraham Lincoln and James Madison

d) James K. Polk and Dwight D. Eisenhower

42. Which President was known for his "Fireside Chats"?

a) Woodrow Wilson

b) Franklin D. Roosevelt

c) Harry S. Truman

d) Dwight D. Eisenhower

43. Which U.S. President appointed the first woman to the Supreme Court?

a) Jimmy Carter

b) Ronald Reagan

c) George H.W. Bush

d) Bill Clinton

44. Who was the first President to be inaugurated in Washington, D.C.?

a) George Washington

b) John Adams

c) Thomas Jefferson

d) James Madison

45. Which President signed the Social Security Act into law?

a) Herbert Hoover

b) Franklin D. Roosevelt

c) Harry S. Truman

d) Dwight D. Eisenhower

46. Which U.S. President once served as a lifeguard and rescued 77 people?

a) John F. Kennedy

b) Lyndon B. Johnson

c) Richard Nixon

d) Ronald Reagan

47. Which President was a Rhodes Scholar?

a) George H.W. Bush

b) Bill Clinton

c) Barack Obama

d) Donald Trump

48. Before taking office, this president had worked as a model and appeared on the cover of Cosmopolitan magazine in his Navy uniform.

a) John F. Kennedy

b) Gerald Ford

c) Ronald Reagan

d) Bill Clinton

49. Which President signed the Affordable Care Act into law?

a) George W. Bush

b) Barack Obama

c) Bill Clinton

d) Joe Biden

50. Which U.S. President served as Vice President under Dwight D. Eisenhower?

a) Richard Nixon

b) Lyndon B. Johnson

c) Harry S. Truman

d) Gerald Ford

Answers:

1. b) Abraham Lincoln

2. b) John Adams

3. c) Thomas Jefferson

4. a) Ronald Reagan

5. b) Theodore Roosevelt

6. b) John F. Kennedy

7. b) Donald Trump

8. b) Franklin D. Roosevelt

9. a) Richard Nixon

10. a) Theodore Roosevelt

11. c) Abraham Lincoln

12. c) John F. Kennedy

13. a) Franklin D. Roosevelt

14. b) Lyndon B. Johnson

15. a) Grover Cleveland

16. b) Zachary Taylor

17. c) Theodore Roosevelt

18. b) Theodore Roosevelt

19. a) Andrew Jackson

20. c) Jimmy Carter

21. b) John F. Kennedy

22. b) George W. Bush

23. c) Thomas Jefferson

24. c) George W. Bush

25. a) George Washington

26. b) Woodrow Wilson

27. c) James Monroe

28. b) Richard Nixon

29. c) Jimmy Carter

30. a) Richard Nixon

31. b) Bill Clinton

32. c) Joe Biden

33. b) Ronald Reagan

34. a) William Henry Harrison

35. c) George H.W. Bush

36. a) George H.W. Bush

37. b) Jimmy Carter

38. d) Theodore Roosevelt

39. b) John F. Kennedy

40. a) John Quincy Adams

41. c) Abraham Lincoln and James Madison

42. b) Franklin D. Roosevelt

43. b) Ronald Reagan

44. c) Thomas Jefferson

45. b) Franklin D. Roosevelt

46. d) Ronald Reagan

47. b) Bill Clinton

48. b) Gerald Ford

49. b) Barack Obama

50. a) Richard Nixon

Chapter 3

The First Ladies of the United States

1. Who was the first First Lady to be born in the United States?

   a) Martha Washington

   b) Abigail Adams

   c) Dolley Madison

   d) Elizabeth Monroe

2. Which First Lady was known for her "Let's Move!" campaign to promote healthy eating and exercise?

   a) Laura Bush

   b) Michelle Obama

   c) Hillary Clinton

   d) Melania Trump

3. Who was the First Lady during the War of 1812, known for saving important artifacts from the White House before the British burned it down?

   a) Martha Washington

   b) Abigail Adams

   c) Dolley Madison

   d) Elizabeth Monroe

4. Which First Lady was known for her "Just Say No" anti-drug campaign?

   a) Betty Ford

   b) Rosalynn Carter

   c) Nancy Reagan

   d) Barbara Bush

5. Who was the First Lady who organized the first White House Easter Egg Roll?

a) Jackie Kennedy

b) Eleanor Roosevelt

c) Bess Truman

d) Lucy Hayes

6. Which First Lady was the first to receive a graduate degree?

a) Lucy Hayes

b) Edith Wilson

c) Frances Cleveland

d) Hillary Clinton

7. Who was the First Lady known for her work with the Red Cross and her advocacy for military families? She was also the first First Lady to fly in an airplane and to hold a regular press conference.

a) Mamie Eisenhower

b) Eleanor Roosevelt

c) Rosalynn Carter

d) Betty Ford

8. Which First Lady was a famous actress before becoming First Lady?

a) Jacqueline Kennedy

b) Nancy Reagan

c) Laura Bush

d) Michelle Obama

9. Who was the First Lady during the Great Depression and World War II?

a) Florence Harding

b) Eleanor Roosevelt

c) Bess Truman

d) Mamie Eisenhower

10. Which First Lady was known for her elegant style and love of the arts? This First Lady was the first to be the mother of an infant in the White House since the turn of the century.

　a) Jackie Kennedy

　b) Nancy Reagan

　c) Barbara Bush

　d) Rosalynn Carter

11. Who was the First Lady that served during both the Civil War and the Reconstruction Era? She was 10 years younger than her husband, who called her by the nickname "Molly".

　a) Mary Todd Lincoln

　b) Edith Wilson

　c) Lucy Hayes

　d) Dolley Madison

12. This First Lady was known for her signature short bangs which women often imitated. She was famous for her adoration of the color pink, which she incorporated into her clothing, accessories and home décor. Even in the White House, she clipped coupons and published a famous fudge recipe.

　a) Jackie Kennedy

　b) Mamie Eisenhower

　c) Bess Truman

　d) Nancy Reagan

13. Who was the First Lady who established the National Foundation for Infantile Paralysis, now known as the March of Dimes?

   a) Eleanor Roosevelt

   b) Betty Ford

   c) Jacqueline Kennedy

   d) Rosalynn Carter

14. Which First Lady was known for her work in promoting literacy and education? She was a second-grade teacher and was a key advocate for the historic education reform, No Child Left Behind Act.

   a) Barbara Bush

   b) Laura Bush

   c) Michelle Obama

   d) Hillary Clinton

15. Who was the First Lady when the United States celebrated its bicentennial in 1976?

   a) Betty Ford

   b) Pat Nixon

   c) Rosalynn Carter

   d) Nancy Reagan

16. Which First Lady was the first to be a professional career woman before becoming First Lady? She was a schoolteacher and established the first White House Library.

   a) Abigail Fillmore

   b) Hillary Clinton

   c) Michelle Obama

   d) Nancy Reagan

17. Who was the First Lady who created the White House Rose Garden?

   a) Jacqueline Kennedy

   b) Ellen Axson Wilson

   c) Lady Bird Johnson

   d) Pat Nixon

18. Which First Lady served as the wife of the only U.S. President to serve two non-consecutive terms?

   a) Frances Cleveland

   b) Ellen Wilson

   c) Bess Truman

   d) Mary Todd Lincoln

19. Who was the First Lady during the signing of the Camp David Accords?

   a) Barbara Bush

   b) Nancy Reagan

   c) Rosalynn Carter

   d) Jackie Kennedy

20. Which First Lady was the first to use the title "First Lady" in a public address?

   a) Dolley Madison

   b) Mary Todd Lincoln

   c) Lucy Hayes

   d) Edith Roosevelt

21. Which First Lady was known for her work on mental health issues and founded the Betty Ford Center?

   a) Betty Ford

   b) Nancy Reagan

   c) Rosalynn Carter

   d) Laura Bush

22. Who was the First Lady who became a U.S. Senator after leaving the White House?

   a) Laura Bush

   b) Hillary Clinton

   c) Michelle Obama

   d) Barbara Bush

23. Which First Lady was known for her contributions to the preservation of American historic sites and furniture? She was instrumental in the fight to save Grand Central Station in NYC.

   a) Jacqueline Kennedy

   b) Edith Wilson

   c) Rosalynn Carter

   d) Nancy Reagan

24. Who was the First Lady when the 19th Amendment, granting women the right to vote, was ratified? She is known as the "Secret President" and "the first woman to run the country" when her husband suffered a prolonged and disabling illness while in office.

   a) Edith Wilson

   b) Florence Harding

   c) Grace Coolidge

d) Eleanor Roosevelt

25. Which First Lady was known for her campaign to beautify the highways and promote environmental conservation? She advocated for the "Highway Beautification Act". She was known as a shrewd investor and manager. She was a primary stockholder in Bell Helicopter Textron.

   a) Pat Nixon

   b) Lady Bird Johnson

   c) Barbara Bush

   d) Michelle Obama

26. This First Lady runs five miles, five times a week. She has her doctoral degree in education and is a lifelong educator.

   a) Jill Biden

   b) Rosalynn Carter

   c) Betty Ford

   d) Nancy Reagan

27. Which First Lady was the first to have her own office in the White House? She is the longest serving First Lady. Remember her famous quote, "The future belongs to those who believe in the beauty of their dreams".

   a) Jackie Kennedy

   b) Eleanor Roosevelt

   c) Edith Wilson

   d) Mamie Eisenhower

28. Who was the First Lady who successfully had a one-lane bowling alley built in the White House?

a) Laura Bush

b) Thelma "Pat" Nixon

c) Jackie Kennedy

d) Bess Truman

29. Which First Lady was the wife of a President who was impeached?

a) Hillary Clinton

b) Nancy Reagan

c) Betty Ford

d) Rosalynn Carter

30. Which First Lady was first to publicly decorate The White House for Halloween in 1958?

a) Helen Taft

b) Eleanor Roosevelt

c) Mamie Eisenhower

d) Grace Coolidge

31. Which First Lady is known for her contributions to the National Endowment for the Arts? She also appeared in a movie "Hellcats of the Navy", opposite her husband.

a) Nancy Reagan

b) Laura Bush

c) Rosalynn Carter

d) Jacqueline Kennedy

32. Who was the First Lady who held the first press conference for a First Lady in U.S. history?

a) Jackie Kennedy

b) Eleanor Roosevelt

c) Nancy Reagan

d) Laura Bush

33. This First Lady had much influence over her husband who gave her the nickname, "The Boss". She was the Honorary President of the Girl Scouts and the American Red Cross. She preferred to keep a low profile as First Lady and avoided the public eye. She didn't hold weekly press conferences and only answered written questions.

   a) Laura Bush

   b) Rosalynn Carter

   c) Bess Truman

   d) Nancy Reagan

34. Who was the First Lady during the Cuban Missile Crisis?

   a) Pat Nixon

   b) Jacqueline Kennedy

   c) Barbara Bush

   d) Nancy Reagan

35. Which First Lady was a famous poet and writer before marrying the President? (Hint: she was the second wife of the 28th President)

   a) Grace Coolidge

   b) Edith Wilson

   c) Jacqueline Kennedy

   d) Helen Taft

36. Who was the First Lady who supported and campaigned for the passage of the Civil Rights Act of 1964? This First Lady traveled to 8 southern states in 1964 promoting the Civil Rights Act. This was the first solo whistle-stop tour by a First Lady. She refused to stay in segregated hotels and was the only woman present when her husband signed the Civil Rights Act.

   a) Lady Bird Johnson

   b) Betty Ford

   c) Barbara Bush

   d) Rosalynn Carter

37. Which First Lady was the first to travel abroad with her husband while he was in office? Her middle name is "Kermit", and she was the First Lady to her childhood companion and the 26th President.

   a) Edith Roosevelt

   b) Jacqueline Kennedy

   c) Nancy Reagan

   d) Michelle Obama

38. Who was the First Lady who was an accomplished artist and designed the White House China? She founded the White House China Collection. This remarkable First Lady worked to expand women's influence outside the home in the late 1800s.

   a) Caroline Harrison

   b) Bess Truman

   c) Edith Wilson

   d) Laura Bush

39. Which First Lady was known for her activism on behalf of disabled veterans and children with disabilities? Not only did she coin a famous quote about 'Caregivers', but she also founded an Institute for Caring.

a) Laura Bush

b) Rosalynn Carter

c) Michelle Obama

d) Nancy Reagan

40. Who was the First Lady during the end of the Cold War?

a) Barbara Bush

b) Nancy Reagan

c) Rosalynn Carter

d) Jacqueline Kennedy

41. Which First Lady was known for her life-changing quotes? One of her most famed quotes being: "No one can make you feel inferior without your consent" and "Women are like teabags. You don't know how strong they are until you put them in hot water".

a) Eleanor Roosevelt

b) Edith Wilson

c) Mary Todd Lincoln

d) Frances Cleveland

42. Who was the First Lady who was the first to host a televised tour of the White House?

a) Jackie Kennedy

b) Nancy Reagan

c) Barbara Bush

d) Michelle Obama

43. Who was the first presidential wife to wear pants in public in the 1970s?

a) Pat Nixon

b) Betty Ford

c) Rosalynn Carter

d) Laura Bush

44. Who was the First Lady who established the National Commission on the Observance of International Women's Year? She was a passionate supporter of the Equal Rights Amendment (ERA).

a) Betty Ford

b) Rosalynn Carter

c) Eleanor Roosevelt

d) Michelle Obama

45. Which First Lady had six children, and was known for her frugal sense of fashion? She was famously known for wearing fake pearls, once humorously disclosing she wore pearl necklaces to hide the wrinkles in her neck. She has written several books and died at the age of 92.

a) Laura Bush

b) Lady Bird Johnson

c) Barbara Bush

d) Michelle Obama

46. Who was the First Lady who was an outspoken advocate for health care reform and children's rights? Together with Janet Reno, this First Lady helped create the Office of Violence Against Women at the Department of Justice.

a) Hillary Clinton

b) Barbara Bush

c) Rosalynn Carter

d) Michelle Obama

47. Who was the only First Lady to appear on U.S. Currency?

   a) Mary Todd Lincoln

   b) Nancy Reagan

   c) Rosalynn Carter

   d) Martha Washington

48. Who was the First Lady during the signing of the Strategic Arms Limitation Talks (SALT) agreement? This First Lady had a nickname of "Queen _____" regarding her taste for splendor.

   a) Barbara Bush

   b) Nancy Reagan

   c) Rosalynn Carter

   d) Jacqueline Kennedy

49. This First Lady was a wealthy widow before marrying her husband who would be President. During the Revolutionary War, she spent winters with her husband at military encampments, making socks for the soldiers. She was known for her needlework, including darning, embroidering and knitting.

   a) Abigail Adams

   b) Mamie Eisenhower

   c) Sarah Polk

   d) Martha Washington

50. Who was the First Lady who worked to expand opportunities for women in business and government? This First Lady majored in political science at Wellesley College, where she graduated with honors in 1969.

   a) Laura Bush

b) Hillary Clinton

c) Michelle Obama

d) Barbara Bush

Answers:

1. b) Abigail Adams

2. b) Michelle Obama

3. c) Dolley Madison

4. c) Nancy Reagan

5. d) Lucy Hayes

6. d) Hillary Clinton

7. b) Eleanor Roosevelt

8. b) Nancy Reagan

9. b) Eleanor Roosevelt

10. a) Jackie Kennedy

11. a) Mary Todd Lincoln

12. b) Mamie Eisenhower

13. a) Eleanor Roosevelt

14. b) Laura Bush

15. a) Betty Ford

16. a) Abigail Fillmore

17. b) Ellen Wilson

18. a) Frances Cleveland

19. c) Rosalynn Carter

20. b) Mary Todd Lincoln

21. a) Betty Ford

22. b) Hillary Clinton

23. a) Jacqueline Kennedy

24. a) Edith Wilson

25. b) Lady Bird Johnson

26. a) Jill Biden

27. b) Eleanor Roosevelt

28. b) Thelma "Pat" Nixon

29. a) Hillary Clinton

30. c) Mamie Eisenhower

31. a) Nancy Reagan

32. b) Eleanor Roosevelt

33. c) Bess Truman

34. b) Jacqueline Kennedy

35. b) Edith Wilson

36. a) Lady Bird Johnson

37. a) Edith Roosevelt

38. a) Caroline Harrison

39. b) Rosalynn Carter

40. b) Nancy Reagan

41. a) Eleanor Roosevelt

42. a) Jackie Kennedy

43. a) Pat NIxon

44. a) Betty Ford

45. c) Barbara Bush

46. a) Hillary Clinton

47. d) Martha Washington

48. b) Nancy Reagan

49. d) Martha Washington

50. b) Hillary Clinton

Chapter 4

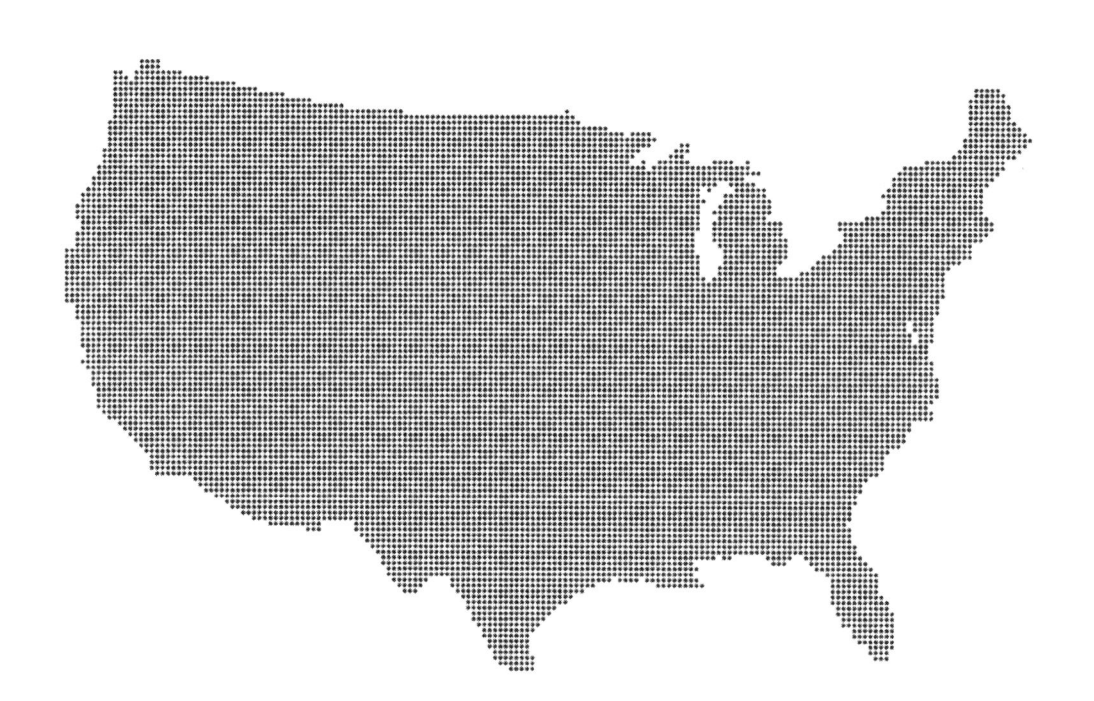

<u>The 50 States</u>

1. Which state is known as the "Sunflower State"?

   a) California

   b) Texas

   c) Kansas

   d) Arizona

2. What is the smallest state by area?

   a) Rhode Island

   b) Delaware

   c) Connecticut

   d) New Hampshire

3. Which state is famous for its potatoes?

   a) Idaho

   b) Maine

   c) Wisconsin

   d) Oregon

4. Which state is home to the Grand Canyon?

   a) Utah

   b) Colorado

   c) Nevada

   d) Arizona

5. What state is known as the "Empire State"?

   a) New Jersey

b) New York

   c) Illinois

   d) Pennsylvania

6. Which state has the nickname "The Aloha State"?

   a) California

   b) Florida

   c) Hawaii

   d) Texas

7. Which state is known for its famous jazz music and Mardi Gras celebrations?

   a) Texas

   b) Louisiana

   c) Mississippi

   d) Alabama

8. Which state is the only state to have a single syllable name?

   a) Maine

   b) Texas

   c) Utah

   d) Georgia

9. What state is known as the "Hawkeye State"?

   a) Minnesota

   b) Michigan

   c) Wisconsin

d) Iowa

10. Which state is famous for its maple syrup production?

   a) Vermont

   b) New Hampshire

   c) Massachusetts

   d) Maine

11. What state is known for its "Hoosiers"?

   a) Indiana

   b) Ohio

   c) Kentucky

   d) Illinois

12. Which state is known as "The Garden State"?

   a) New York

   b) New Jersey

   c) Pennsylvania

   d) Connecticut

13. Which state is known for its beautiful coastline and vineyards, and is often associated with wine production?

   a) Oregon

   b) Washington

   c) California

   d) Hawaii

14. Which state is the only U.S. state that was once an independent country?

   a) Texas

   b) California

   c) Florida

   d) Hawaii

15. Which state is home to the largest hot spring in the U.S.?

   a) Arkansas

   b) Montana

   c) Wyoming

   d) Colorado

16. What state is famous for its "Space Needle"?

   a) Oregon

   b) Washington

   c) California

   d) Nevada

17. Which state is known for the famous "Mount Rushmore"?

   a) South Dakota

   b) North Dakota

   c) Montana

   d) Wyoming

18. Which state is the birthplace of country music?

a) Texas

b) Virginia

c) Tennessee

d) New York

19. Which state is known for its large number of wineries and is often called "Wine Country"?

a) Oregon

b) New York

c) California

d) Virginia

20. What state is famous for its annual "Kentucky Derby" horse race?

a) Kentucky

b) Tennessee

c) Ohio

d) Virginia

21. Which state is known as "The Last Frontier"?

a) Montana

b) Alaska

c) Wyoming

d) Idaho

22. Which state has the nickname "The Silver State"?

a) Colorado

b) Nevada

c) California

d) Utah

23. Which state is the leading producer of soybeans in the U.S.?

   a) Iowa

   b) Illinois

   c) Indiana

   d) Nebraska

24. Which state is famous for its annual "Sturgis Motorcycle Rally"?

   a) South Dakota

   b) North Dakota

   c) Nebraska

   d) Montana

25. What state is home to the famous "Mammoth Cave National Park"?

   a) Kentucky

   b) Tennessee

   c) Virginia

   d) West Virginia

26. Which state is known for its annual "Albuquerque International Balloon Fiesta"?

   a) Texas

   b) Arizona

   c) New Mexico

d) Utah

27. Which state is famous for the creation of "Spam" meat?

   a) Iowa

   b) Minnesota

   c) Wisconsin

   d) Michigan

28. Which state is the largest in terms of land area?

   a) Texas

   b) California

   c) Alaska

   d) Montana

29. What state is known as "The Beaver State"?

   a) Oregon

   b) Washington

   c) Idaho

   d) Nevada

30. Which state is known for having the largest number farms?

   a) California

   b) Texas

   c) Colorado

   d) Alaska

31. Which state is the smallest by population?

   a) Vermont

   b) New Hampshire

   c) Rhode Island

   d) Wyoming

32. Which state is famous for its historic Plymouth Rock?

   a) Massachusetts

   b) Rhode Island

   c) Connecticut

   d) New Hampshire

33. Which state has the nickname "The Sunshine State"?

   a) California

   b) Texas

   c) Florida

   d) Arizona

34. Which state is home to the famous "Gateway Arch"?

   a) Missouri

   b) Montana

   c) Idaho

   d) Colorado

35. Which state is known for its annual "Tulip Festival"?

   a) Oregon

b) Washington

c) Michigan

d) Ohio

36. Which state is known for having the most corn?

    a) Hawaii

    b) Minnesota

    c) Iowa

    d) Oregon

37. Which state is the leading producer of cotton in the U.S.?

    a) Texas

    b) Alabama

    c) Georgia

    d) Mississippi

38. Which state is known for its annual "Sundance Film Festival"?

    a) Colorado

    b) Utah

    c) Nevada

    d) California

39. Which state is famous for its "Mount Olympus"?

    a) California

    b) Ohio

    c) Massachusetts

d) Washington

40. Which state is known for having the most trees?

   a) Maine

   b) Minnesota

   c) Wisconsin

   d) Vermont

41. Which state is famous for its "Hoover Dam"?

   a) Arizona

   b) Nevada

   c) Utah

   d) a and b

42. Which state has the nickname "The Pine Tree State"?

   a) New Hampshire

   b) Vermont

   c) Maine

   d) Massachusetts

43. Which state is known for the "Lone Star State"?

   a) Nevada

   b) Utah

   c) Colorado

   d) Texas

44. Which state is famous for its vast prairies, rolling plains, college football, its pioneer history and the development of Kool-Aid?

 a) Wyoming

 b) Oklahoma

 c) Nebraska

 d) Nevada

45. Which state is the leading producer of cranberries in the U.S.?

 a) Massachusetts

 b) Wisconsin

 c) New Jersey

 d) Michigan

46. Which state is known for the famous "Niagara Falls"?

 a) New York

 b) Michigan

 c) Pennsylvania

 d) Ohio

47. Which state is the leading producer of peaches?

 a) South Carolina

 b) Georgia

 c) California

 d) Florida

48. Which state is known for its "Hollywood" district?

a) New York

b) California

c) Florida

d) Nevada

49. Which state is the top apple-producing state?

a) Washington

b) California

c) Hawaii

d) Oregon

50. Which state is known for its "Rocky Mountains"?

a) Colorado

b) Utah

c) Wyoming

d) Montana

Answers:

1. c) Kansas

2. a) Rhode Island

3. a) Idaho

4. d) Arizona

5. b) New York

6. c) Hawaii

7. b) Louisiana

8. a) Maine

9. d) Iowa

10. a) Vermont

11. a) Indiana

12. b) New Jersey

13. c) California

14. a) Texas

15. c) Wyoming

16. b) Washington

17. a) South Dakota

18. b) Virginia

19. c) California

20. a) Kentucky

21. b) Alaska

22. b) Nevada

23. b) Illinois

24. a) South Dakota

25. a) Kentucky

26. c) New Mexico

27. b) Minnesota

28. c) Alaska

29. a) Oregon

30. b) Texas

31. d) Wyoming

32. a) Massachusetts

33. c) Florida

34. a) Missouri

35. b) Washington

36. c) Iowa

37. a) Texas

38. b) Utah

39. d) Washington

40. a) Maine

41. d) Arizona and Nevada

42. c) Maine

43. d) Texas

44. c) Nebraska

45. b) Wisconsin

46. a) New York

47. b) Georgia

48. b) California

49. a) Washington

50. a) Colorado

Chapter 5

U.S. Geography

1. Which state has the longest coastline?

   a) California

   b) Alaska

   c) Florida

   d) Texas

2. Which state is home to the Great Salt Lake?

   a) Colorado

   b) Idaho

   c) Utah

   d) Wyoming

3. Which U.S. state has the most volcanoes?

   a) California

   b) Alaska

   c) Washington

   d) Oregon

4. Which state is known for having the lowest elevation in the U.S.?

   a) Nevada

   b) California

   c) Florida

   d) Louisiana

5. Which state is the only one to have a coastline on both the Arctic and Pacific Oceans?

   a) Oregon

b) California

c) Washington

d) Alaska

6. Which state is the largest by land area?

    a) Texas

    b) California

    c) Alaska

    d) Montana

7. Which state is known for its famous "Mammoth Cave"?

    a) Tennessee

    b) Kentucky

    c) West Virginia

    d) Virginia

8. Which state is home to the highest peak in the contiguous United States?

    a) Colorado

    b) Wyoming

    c) Utah

    d) California

9. Which state is the birthplace of the Mississippi River?

    a) Missouri

    b) Minnesota

    c) Iowa

d) Illinois

10. Which state has the largest freshwater lake by surface area in the U.S.?

   a) Michigan

   b) Florida

   c) Minnesota

   d) New York

11. Which U.S. state has the most mountain ranges?

   a) Montana

   b) Colorado

   c) Alaska

   d) Nevada

12. Which state is known for the famous "Death Valley"?

   a) Nevada

   b) Utah

   c) California

   d) Arizona

13. Which state is home to the city of Ann Arbor?

   a) Indiana

   b) Michigan

   c) Ohio

   d) Illinois

14. Which state is bordered by Canada to the north and has the longest border with Canada?

   a) New York

   b) Alaska

   c) Michigan

   d) Minnesota

15. Which state is known for its extensive cave systems, including the "Carlsbad Caverns"?

   a) Texas

   b) New Mexico

   c) Kentucky

   d) Tennessee

16. Which state is known for the "Everglades National Park"?

   a) Georgia

   b) Alabama

   c) Florida

   d) South Carolina

17. Which state has the largest number of national parks?

   a) Utah

   b) California

   c) Alaska

   d) Colorado

18. Which state is home to the "Rocky Mountains"?

a) Colorado

   b) Wyoming

   c) Montana

   d) All of the above

19. Which state is famous for The Statue of Liberty?

    a) New York

    b) Hawaii

    c) Florida

    d) Texas

20. Which state has the most lakes?

    a) Alaska

    b) Michigan

    c) Wisconsin

    d) Vermont

21. Which state is known for the "Yellowstone National Park"?

    a) Wyoming

    b) Montana

    c) Idaho

    d) Utah

22. Which state is known for the "Maui" island?

    a) California

    b) Hawaii

c) Florida

d) Texas

23. Which state is the only one to have a coastline on the Gulf of Mexico and the Atlantic Ocean?

   a) Louisiana

   b) Florida

   c) Texas

   d) Alabama

24. Which state is famous for its "Sequoia National Park"?

   a) Oregon

   b) California

   c) Washington

   d) Nevada

25. Which state has the highest average elevation?

   a) Colorado

   b) Utah

   c) New Mexico

   d) Wyoming

26. Which state is home to the "Great Smoky Mountains"?

   a) Kentucky

   b) North Carolina

   c) Tennessee

d) b and c

27. Which state is known for the "Gulf Shores"?

   a) Mississippi

   b) Alabama

   c) Florida

   d) Louisiana

28. Which state is home to the "Badlands National Park"?

   a) South Dakota

   b) North Dakota

   c) Montana

   d) Nebraska

29. Which state is known for having the largest national forests?

   a) Oregon

   b) Washington

   c) California

   d) Alaska

30. What is the name of the highest peak in the contiguous U.S. (which is in California)?

   a) Mount Vernon

   b) Mount Whitney

   c) Mount Everest

   d) Rocky Mountain

31. The Missouri River begins in this state.

   a) Illinois

   b) Montana

   c) Minnesota

   d) Missouri

32. Which state is known for its "Lava Beds National Monument"?

   a) Idaho

   b) California

   c) Nevada

   d) Oregon

33. Which state is home to the "Grand Tetons"?

   a) Wyoming

   b) Montana

   c) Utah

   d) Idaho

34. Which state is known for its "Appalachian Mountains"?

   a) West Virginia

   b) North Carolina

   c) Tennessee

   d) All of the above

35. Which state is known for the "Charles River"?

   a) Massachusetts

b) New Jersey

c) New York

d) Pennsylvania

36. Which state is known for the "Haleakalā National Park"?

    a) California

    b) Texas

    c) Hawaii

    d) Nevada

37. Which state has the highest point east of the Mississippi River?

    a) North Carolina

    b) Virginia

    c) Georgia

    d) Tennessee

38. Which state is known for the "Arches National Park"?

    a) Colorado

    b) Arizona

    c) Utah

    d) Nevada

39. Which state is famous for its "Windy City"?

    a) Michigan

    b) Ohio

    c) Illinois

d) Indiana

40. Which state is known for its "Great Dismal Swamp"?

   a) Virginia

   b) North Carolina

   c) South Carolina

   d) a and b

41. Which state is home to the "Liberty Bell"?

   a) New York

   b) New Jersey

   c) Pennsylvania

   d) Massachusetts

42. Which state has the largest urban park system?

   a) Arizona

   b) California

   c) Texas

   d) Alaska

43. Which state is known for its "Mason-Dixon Line"?

   a) Maryland

   b) Pennsylvania

   c) a and b

   d) Delaware

44. Which state has the largest sand dunes in North America?

   a) New Mexico

   b) Colorado

   c) California

   d) Texas

45. Which state is famous for its "Yosemite National Park"?

   a) Nevada

   b) California

   c) Utah

   d) Colorado

46. Which U.S. River is the dirtiest river and has the nickname "The Big Muddy"?

   a) Minnesota

   b) Mississippi

   c) Missouri

   d) Hudson

47. A pilot named "Sully" expertly landed a plane atop what famous river in New York State?

   a) Delaware River

   b) Susquehanna River

   c) Penobscot River

   d) Hudson River

48. This state is known for its famous canyon named "Hells Canyon" which is the deepest gorge in North America, and is even deeper that the Grand Canyon.

a) Idaho

b) Alaska

c) Montana

d) Washington

49. Which state is known for having the "Most Populous City" in the U.S.?

   a) California

   b) Texas

   c) New York

   d) Florida

50. Which state has the "Gila Monster" as its state reptile?

   a) Arizona

   b) New Mexico

   c) Nevada

   d) Utah

Answers:

1. b) Alaska
2. c) Utah
3. b) Alaska
4. d) Louisiana
5. d) Alaska
6. c) Alaska
7. b) Kentucky
8. d) California
9. b) Minnesota
10. a) Michigan
11. d) Nevada
12. c) California
13. b) Michigan
14. b) Alaska
15. b) New Mexico
16. c) Florida
17. b) California
18. d) All of the above
19. a) New York
20. a) Alaska
21. a) Wyoming
22. b) Hawaii
23. b) Florida
24. b) California
25. a) Colorado

26. d) North Carolina and Tennessee

27. b) Alabama

28. a) South Dakota

29. d) Alaska

30. b) Mount Whitney

31. b) Montana

32. b) California

33. a) Wyoming

34. d) All of the above

35. a) Massachusetts

36. c) Hawaii

37. a) North Carolina

38. c) Utah

39. c) Illinois

40. d) a and b - Virginia and North Carolina

41. c) Pennsylvania

42. d) Alaska

43. c) Maryland and Pennsylvania

44. b) Colorado

45. b) California

46. b) Mississippi

47. d) Hudson River

48. a) Idaho

49. c) New York

50. d) Utah

Chapter 6

<u>American Revolutionary War</u>

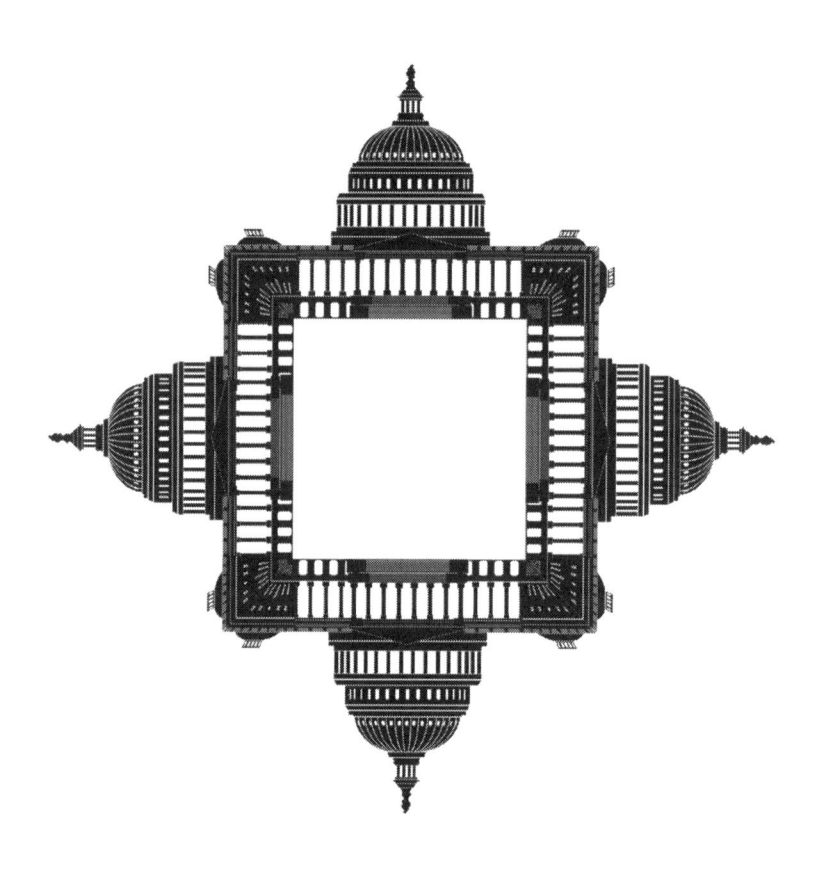

1. Who was the commander-in-chief of the Continental Army during the American Revolutionary War?

   a) Thomas Jefferson

   b) Benjamin Franklin

   c) George Washington

   d) John Adams

2. Which battle is considered the turning point of the American Revolutionary War?

   a) Battle of Bunker Hill

   b) Battle of Saratoga

   c) Battle of Yorktown

   d) Battle of Trenton

3. Who was the main author of the Declaration of Independence?

   a) John Adams

   b) Benjamin Franklin

   c) Thomas Jefferson

   d) James Madison

4. Which country provided significant military support to the American colonies during the Revolutionary War?

   a) Spain

   b) France

   c) Netherlands

   d) Prussia

5. What was the name of the treaty that ended the American Revolutionary War?

a) Treaty of Paris

b) Treaty of Versailles

c) Treaty of Ghent

d) Treaty of Utrecht

6. Which American general is known for his betrayal and defection to the British side?

a) Benedict Arnold

b) Nathaniel Greene

c) Henry Knox

d) Daniel Morgan

7. Where did George Washington famously cross the Delaware River on Christmas night in 1776?

a) New York

b) New Jersey

c) Pennsylvania

d) Massachusetts

8. What are the first 10 amendments to the US Constitution which were adopted as a single unit on December 15, 1791?

a) The Bill of Rights

b) The Federalist Papers

c) The Declaration of Independence

d) The Articles of Confederation

9. Which battle marked the end of major fighting in the American Revolutionary War?

a) Battle of Yorktown

b) Battle of Lexington and Concord

c) Battle of Bunker Hill

d) Battle of Kings Mountain

10. Who was the British commander who surrendered at the Battle of Yorktown?

a) General Cornwallis

b) General Howe

c) General Clinton

d) General Burgoyne

11. Which founding father was known for his role as a diplomat and negotiating crucial aid from France? (Hint- his most famous pen name was Richard Saunders)

a) John Jay

b) Benjamin Franklin

c) Alexander Hamilton

d) Thomas Jefferson

12. What was the date the Treaty of Paris was signed ending the American Revolutionary War?

a) September 3, 1783

b) July 4, 1776

c) August 2, 1776

d) February 22, 1732

13. What was the primary objective of the Continental Army's winter at Valley Forge in 1777-1778?

a) To recruit new soldiers

b) To train and regroup

c) To negotiate with the British

d) To capture a strategic fort

14. Who wrote the influential pamphlet "Common Sense" that advocated for American independence?

a) Thomas Paine

b) John Locke

c) Benjamin Franklin

d) Samuel Adams

15. Which American naval commander is famous for his victory over the British in the Battle of Flamborough Head?

a) John Paul Jones

b) Benedict Arnold

c) George Rogers Clark

d) Richard Henry Lee

16. Which act passed by the British Parliament in 1773 led to the Boston Tea Party?

a) Stamp Act

b) Townshend Acts

c) Tea Act

d) Intolerable Acts

17. Which colonial leader was known for his role in the Boston Tea Party and as a radical patriot?

a) Samuel Adams

b) John Adams

c) Paul Revere

d) Thomas Jefferson

18. Which American general is known for his leadership at the Battle of Bunker Hill?

   a) George Washington

   b) William Prescott

   c) Nathaniel Greene

   d) Benedict Arnold

19. Which battle was the first major conflict of the American Revolutionary War?

   a) Battle of Yorktown

   b) Battle of Lexington and Concord

   c) Battle of Bunker Hill

   d) Battle of Trenton

20. This battle was small but pivotal in the American Revolutionary War on the morning of December 26, 1776, in New Jersey.

   a) Battle of Yorktown

   b) Battle of Trenton

   c) Battle of Saratoga

   d) Battle of Kings Mountain

21. Which American general was known for his leadership in the Southern campaign and his victory at the Battle of Cowpens?

   a) Daniel Morgan

   b) Nathaniel Greene

c) Benedict Arnold

d) George Rogers Clark

22. What event was a direct response to the British attempt to enforce the Quartering Act?

a) Boston Massacre

b) Boston Tea Party

c) Intolerable Acts

d) Lexington and Concord

23. Which act required colonists to provide housing and supplies for British troops?

a) Stamp Act

b) Quartering Act

c) Townshend Acts

d) Tea Act

24. Who was the British Prime Minister who was a key figure in the lead-up to the American Revolution?

a) William Pitt

b) George Grenville

c) Lord North

d) Charles Townshend

25. Which battle was significant for its outcome and led to the formal alliance between France and the American colonies?

a) Battle of Yorktown

b) Battle of Saratoga

c) Battle of Trenton

d) Battle of Bunker Hill

26. Which famous American inventor and patriot is known for his role in the Continental Congress and his contributions to science and diplomacy?

   a) Benjamin Franklin

   b) Thomas Jefferson

   c) John Adams

   d) Alexander Hamilton

27. Which American general is noted for his defense of the fort at Fort Ticonderoga?

   a) Richard Montgomery

   b) Benedict Arnold

   c) George Washington

   d) Nathaniel Greene

28. The Federalist Papers is a collection of 85 articles and essays written by Alexander Hamilton, James Madison, and John Jay written under what pen name?

   a) Boston Tea Partiers

   b) The Federalists

   c) The Revolutionaries

   d) Publius

29. Which British general was defeated at the Battle of Saratoga, leading to American victory and French support?

   a) General Clinton

   b) General Howe

   c) General Burgoyne

d) General Cornwallis

30. What was the purpose of the Continental Congress in 1774?

   a) To draft the Constitution

   b) To address grievances and unite the colonies

   c) To declare independence

   d) To negotiate peace with Britain

31. Which American patriot is famous for his midnight ride to warn of the British approach?

   a) Samuel Adams

   b) Paul Revere

   c) John Hancock

   d) James Madison

32. What was the main purpose of the Olive Branch Petition?

   a) To declare war

   b) To seek peace with Britain

   c) To form a new government

   d) To request foreign aid

33. Which British act-imposed taxes on paper, glass, lead, and tea in the American colonies?

   a) Stamp Act

   b) Townshend Acts

   c) Tea Act

   d) Intolerable Acts

34. Who was the primary author of the U.S. Constitution after the Revolutionary War?

   a) James Madison

   b) George Washington

   c) Thomas Jefferson

   d) Alexander Hamilton

35. Which battle was a decisive victory for the British early in the war and led to the occupation of New York City?

   a) Battle of Bunker Hill

   b) Battle of Trenton

   c) Battle of Long Island

   d) Battle of Yorktown

36. Which document first set forth the American colonies' desire to form a new government separate from Britain?

   a) The Declaration of Independence

   b) The Articles of Confederation

   c) The Federalist Papers

   d) The Magna Carta

37. Which battle involved a surprise attack by Washington and his troops on the Hessian soldiers?

   a) Battle of Saratoga

   b) Battle of Trenton

   c) Battle of Yorktown

   d) Battle of Lexington and Concord

38. American Forces at the Battle of Saratoga was led by which General?

   a) Horatio Gates

   b) Daniel Morgan

   c) William Howe

   d) Benedict Arnold

39. Which American general is credited with the famous quote, "I have not yet begun to fight!"?

   a) John Paul Jones

   b) George Washington

   c) Benedict Arnold

   d) Nathaniel Greene

40. Which American state was the site of the Battle of Bunker Hill?

   a) Massachusetts

   b) New York

   c) Virginia

   d) Pennsylvania

41. Which act was enacted to punish Massachusetts for the Boston Tea Party and included measures such as closing Boston Harbor?

   a) Intolerable Acts

   b) Stamp Act

   c) Tea Act

   d) Quartering Act

42. Which two men famously signed their names prominently on the Declaration of Independence?

   a) John Adams and Thomas Jefferson

   b) Thomas Jefferson and John Hancock

   c) Samuel Adams and Paul Revere

   d) George Washington and James Madison

43. Which American commander is known for his leadership at the Battle of Kings Mountain?

   a) Nathaniel Greene

   b) William Campbell

   c) Benedict Arnold

   d) George Rogers Clark

44. Which American general was known for his use of unconventional tactics and guerilla warfare?

   a) Daniel Morgan

   b) George Washington

   c) Nathaneal Greene

   d) John Paul Jones

45. What major turning point effectively ended major combat in the Revolutionary War?

   a) The signing of the Declaration of Independence

   b) The surrender of General Cornwallis

   c) The Battle of Yorktown

   d) The Treaty of Paris

46. Which group was instrumental in organizing resistance to British policies and played a key role in the American Revolution?

   a) The Sons of Liberty

   b) The Federalists

   c) The Continental Congress

   d) The Loyalists

47. Which battle was a key early victory for the American forces in the southern colonies?

   a) Battle of Yorktown

   b) Battle of Cowpens

   c) Battle of Trenton

   d) Battle of Bunker Hill

48. Which American leader famously said, "Give me liberty, or give me death!"?

   a) Thomas Paine

   b) Patrick Henry

   c) Samuel Adams

   d) George Washington

49. Which act reduced the tax on imported British tea giving British merchants an unfair advantage in selling their tea in America?

   a) Stamp Act

   b) Tea Act

   c) Townshend Acts

   d) Intolerable Acts

50. What was the primary purpose of the Committees of Correspondence?

a) To negotiate with Britain

b) To organize colonial resistance

c) To draft the Constitution

d) To establish a new government

Answers:

1. c) George Washington

2. b) Battle of Saratoga

3. c) Thomas Jefferson

4. b) France

5. a) Treaty of Paris

6. a) Benedict Arnold

7. b) New Jersey

8. a) The Bill of Rights

9. a) Battle of Yorktown

10. a) General Cornwallis

11. b) Benjamin Franklin

12. a) September 3, 1783

13. b) To train and regroup

14. a) Thomas Paine

15. a) John Paul Jones

16. c) Tea Act

17. a) Samuel Adams

18. b) William Prescott

19. b) Battle of Lexington and Concord

20. b) Battle of Trenton

21. a) Daniel Morgan

22. a) Boston Massacre

23. b) Quartering Act

24. c) Lord North

25. b) Battle of Saratoga

26. a) Benjamin Franklin

27. b) Benedict Arnold

28. d) Publius

29. c) General Burgoyne

30. b) To address grievances and unite the colonies

31. b) Paul Revere

32. b) To seek peace with Britain

33. b) Townshend Acts

34. a) James Madison

35. c) Battle of Long Island

36. a) The Declaration of Independence

37. b) Battle of Trenton

38. a) Horatio Gates

39. a) John Paul Jones

40. a) Massachusetts

41. a) Intolerable Acts

42. b) Thomas Jefferson and John Hancock

43. b) William Campbell

44. c) Nathaneal Greene

45. b) The surrender of General Cornwallis

46. a) The Sons of Liberty

47. b) Battle of Cowpens

48. b) Patrick Henry

49. b) Tea Act

50. b) To organize colonial resistance

Chapter 7

American Inventors

1. Who is credited with inventing the light bulb?

   a) Alexander Graham Bell

   b) Thomas Edison

   c) Nikola Tesla

   d) Samuel Morse

2. Which inventor is known for developing the first practical telephone?

   a) Thomas Edison

   b) Alexander Graham Bell

   c) Elisha Otis

   d) Henry Ford

3. Who invented the airplane?

   a) The Wright brothers

   b) Alexander Graham Bell

   c) Samuel Langley

   d) Robert Fulton

4. Which inventor created the first practical electric car?

   a) Thomas Edison

   b) John Logie Baird

   c) William Morrison

   d) Elon Musk

5. Who is known for his contributions to the development of the modern assembly line?

   a) Henry Ford

b) Thomas Edison

c) Nikola Tesla

d) Eli Whitney

6. Which inventor was an electrical engineer who developed FM (frequency modulation) radio? He is known as the "father of FM radio".

   a) Guglielmo Marconi

   b) Nikola Tesla

   c) Edwin Armstrong

   d) Lee De Forest

7. Who invented the first practical and affordable sewing machine?

   a) Elias Howe

   b) Isaac Singer

   c) Samuel Morse

   d) James Watt

8. Which American inventor is known for his work on the electric motor and transformer?

   a) Thomas Edison

   b) Nikola Tesla

   c) Alexander Graham Bell

   d) Michael Faraday

9. Who developed the first successful practical typewriter?

   a) Christopher Sholes

   b) Thomas Edison

c) Elisha Otis

d) Hiram Maxim

10. Which inventor is associated with the development of the modern refrigerator?

   a) John Gorrie

   b) Benjamin Franklin

   c) George Eastman

   d) Thomas Edison

11. Who is known for inventing the modern bowling ball?

   a) Leonardo da Vinci

   b) Joseph Gentiluomo

   c) Grant Morton

   d) Andrew Smith

12. Which inventor is credited with developing the first successful gasoline-powered car?

   a) Henry Ford

   b) Karl Benz

   c) Thomas Edison

   d) Nikola Tesla

13. Who invented the first successful mechanical reaper?

   a) Cyrus McCormick

   b) Eli Whitney

   c) John Deere

   d) George Washington Carver

14. Which inventor is famous for creating the first commercially successful motion picture camera?

   a) Thomas Edison

   b) George Eastman

   c) Louis Le Prince

   d) Samuel Morse

15. Who invented the first commercially successful portable vacuum cleaner?

   a) Hubert Cecil Booth

   b) James Dyson

   c) James Murray Spangler

   d) Thomas Edison

16. Which inventor developed the first practical artificial limb?

   a) Richard K. C. Smith

   b) James Edward Hanger

   c) Thomas Edison

   d) George Washington Carver

17. Who is credited with inventing the first successful automobile electric starter which put an end to the difficult and dangerous practice of hand cranking a car engine?

   a) Henry Ford

   b) Alfred Horner

   c) Charles Kettering

   d) George Westinghouse

18. Which American inventor is known for creating the first successful electric car?

    a) Thomas Edison

    b) Elon Musk

    c) Charles Kettering

    d) William Morrison

19. Who developed the first practical and widely used type of synthetic rubber?

    a) Charles Goodyear

    b) John Dunlop

    c) Richard Arkwright

    d) Elias Howe

20. Which inventor is known for his work on the development of the cotton gin?

    a) Eli Whitney

    b) John Deere

    c) Cyrus McCormick

    d) George Washington Carver

21. Who invented the first practical air conditioner?

    a) Willis Carrier

    b) Benjamin Franklin

    c) Nikola Tesla

    d) Thomas Edison

22. Which inventor is famous for his work on the development of the first successful long-distance telegraph?

a) Samuel Morse

b) Alexander Graham Bell

c) Elisha Gray

d) Michael Faraday

23. Who is known for developing the first instant photography system with the Polaroid Corporation?

a) George Eastman

b) Thomas Edison

c) Louis Lumière

d) Edwin Land

24. Which inventor is associated with the development of the first successful disposable razor?

a) King C. Gillette

b) Thomas Edison

c) Eli Whitney

d) John D. Rockefeller

25. Who invented the first practical electric ceiling fan?

a) Philip Diehl

b) Thomas Edison

c) Nikola Tesla

d) George Washington Carver

26. Who was an American engineer, entrepreneur and medical doctor who invented the first commercially successful personal computer in 1974?

a) Steve Jobs

b) Bill Gates

c) Henry Edward Roberts

d) Charles Babbage

27. Who invented the first successful modern rocket engine?

    a) Robert H. Goddard

    b) Wernher von Braun

    c) Elon Musk

    d) Richard Branson

28. Which inventor is famous for developing the first practical electric razor?

    a) King C. Gillette

    b) Thomas Edison

    c) Joseph Lister

    d) Jacob Schick

29. Who developed the first practical and efficient method for converting crude oil into gasoline?

    a) Edwin Drake

    b) John D. Rockefeller

    c) George Babcock

    d) James Joule

30. Which inventor created the first commercially successful electric washing machine?

    a) Alva Fisher

b) Thomas Edison

   c) James Dyson

   d) George Washington Carver

31. Who is known for inventing the first practical folding wheelchair?

   a) Harry Jennings

   b) John R. Hargrove

   c) George Eastman

   d) Thomas Edison

32. Which inventor is known for his work on the development of the Audion vacuum tube, which made possible live radio broadcasting?

   a) Lee De Forest

   b) Thomas Edison

   c) Alexander Graham Bell

   d) Nikola Tesla

33. Who invented the first practical and widely used method of creating steel from pig iron?

   a) Andrew Carnegie

   b) Henry Bessemer

   c) John A. Roebling

   d) Richard Arkwright

34. Which inventor developed the first practical and widely used can opener?

   a) Ezra J. Warner

   b) Hans Wilsdorf

c) Rolex

d) Thomas Edison

35. Who invented the first successful mechanical clothes dryer?

   a) Alva Fisher

   b) Thomas Edison

   c) George T. Sampson

   d) Henry Ford

36. Which inventor and electrical engineer developed and patented the world's first commercial microwave oven?

   a) Arthur James

   b) Albert M. Smith

   c) George E. Schneider

   d) Percy Spencer

37. Who developed the first practical computer mouse?

   a) Douglas Engelbart

   b) Steve Jobs

   c) Bill Gates

   d) Alan Turing

38. Which American inventor is known for his work on the development of the first successful solar engine?

   a) Frank Shuman

   b) Thomas Edison

   c) George Washington Carver

d) Albert Einstein

39. Who invented the first practical and widely used type of electric heater?

   a) Thomas Edison

   b) Albert Einstein

   c) George Washington Carver

   d) Paul G. Schmidt

40. Which inventor developed the first successful practical gasoline-powered lawnmower?

   a) Edwin Beard Budding

   b) Ransom E. Olds

   c) James A. Wright

   d) Paul Simpson

41. Who invented the first successful practical and portable type of electric power tool?

   a) Black & Decker

   b) Thomas Edison

   c) DeWalt

   d) Bosch

42. Which inventor is known for his work on the development of the first practical radio-controlled vehicle?

   a) Nikola Tesla

   b) Thomas Edison

   c) Guglielmo Marconi

   d) Charles Babbage

43. Who invented the first successful and practical type of artificial heart?

   a) Barney Clark

   b) Robert Jarvik

   c) Michael DeBakey

   d) Paul Winchell

44. Which inventor is famous for inventing swim fins? (Hint-this inventor used Richard Saunders as his pen name)

   a) Jacques Cousteau

   b) Leonardo da Vinci

   c) George Washington Carver

   d) Benjamin Franklin

45. Who invented the first successful solid-body electric guitar in 1941?

   a) Les Paul

   b) Leo Fender

   c) Paul Bigsby

   d) Eddie Van Halen

46. Which American inventor is considered the "father of the modern smartphone"?

   a) Steve Jobs

   b) Nikola Tesla

   c) Thomas Edison

d) James Watt

47. Who is known for inventing the first safe passenger elevator in 1853?

   a) Black & Decker

   b) Thomas Edison

   c) Elisha Graves Otis

   d) Robert Bosch

48. Which inventor created the first practical and widely used automated teller machine (ATM)?

   a) John Shepherd-Barron

   b) Charles Babbage

   c) Thomas Edison

   d) Steve Jobs

49. Who invented the first successful practical and widely used digital computer?

   a) Alan Turing

   b) John Atanasoff

   c) Charles Babbage

   d) Bill Gates

50. Who is the American creator and designer of the Xbox?

   a) Jonathan "Seamus" Blackley

   b) Thomas Edison

   c) George Eastman

   d) John S. Thurman

Answers:

1. b) Thomas Edison

2. b) Alexander Graham Bell

3. a) The Wright brothers

4. c) William Morrison

5. a) Henry Ford

6. c) Edwin Armstrong

7. a) Elias Howe

8. b) Nikola Tesla

9. a) Christopher Sholes

10. a) John Gorrie

11. b) Joseph Gentiluomo

12. b) Karl Benz

13. a) Cyrus McCormick

14. a) Thomas Edison

15. c) James Murray Spangler

16. b) James Edward Hanger

17. c) Charles Kettering

18. d) William Morrison

19. a) Charles Goodyear

20. a) Eli Whitney

21. a) Willis Carrier

22. a) Samuel Morse

23. d) Edwin Land

24. a) King C. Gillette

25. a) Philip Diehl

26. c) Henry Edward Roberts

27. a) Robert H. Goddard

28. d) Jacob Schick

29. a) Edwin Drake

30. a) Alva Fisher

31. a) Harry Jennings

32. a) Lee De Forest

33. b) Henry Bessemer

34. a) Ezra J. Warner

35. c) George T. Sampson

36. d) Percy Spencer

37. a) Douglas Engelbart

38. a) Frank Shuman

39. a) Thomas Edison

40. b) Ransom E. Olds

41. a) Black & Decker

42. a) Nikola Tesla

43. b) Robert Jarvik

44. d) Benjamin Franklin

45. a) Les Paul

46. a) Steve Jobs

47. c) Elisha Graves Otis

48. a) John Shepherd-Barron

49. b) John Atanasoff

50. a) Jonathan "Seamus" Blackley

Chapter 8

American Athletics

1. Who is known as "The Greatest" and was a three-time world heavyweight boxing champion?

   a) Mike Tyson

   b) Floyd Mayweather

   c) Muhammad Ali

   d) Joe Frazier

2. Which female gymnast is known for winning four gold medals in the 2016 Rio Olympics?

   a) Nadia Comaneci

   b) Simone Biles

   c) Gabby Douglas

   d) Mary Lou Retton

3. Who is considered one of the greatest basketball players of all time, winning six NBA championships with the Chicago Bulls?

   a) Magic Johnson

   b) Michael Jordan

   c) LeBron James

   d) Larry Bird

4. Which American swimmer holds the record for the most Olympic gold medals?

   a) Michael Phelps

   b) Ryan Lochte

   c) Mark Spitz

   d) Caeleb Dressel

5. Who is the female tennis player with the most Grand Slam singles titles?

   a) Serena Williams

   b) Steffi Graf

   c) Martina Navratilova

   d) Chris Evert

6. Which American football player is known for his "Hail Mary" pass in the 1975 NFC Championship Game?

   a) Tom Brady

   b) Joe Montana

   c) Brett Favre

   d) Dan Marino

7. Who is the American female track and field athlete known for setting world records in the 100m and 200m sprints?

   a) Florence Griffith-Joyner

   b) Jackie Joyner-Kersee

   c) Allyson Felix

   d) Wilma Rudolph

8. Which baseball player holds the record for the most career home runs?

   a) Hank Aaron

   b) Babe Ruth

   c) Barry Bonds

   d) Willie Mays

9. Who is the American skier who won four gold medals in the 2002 Salt Lake City Winter Olympics?

   a) Lindsey Vonn

   b) Bode Miller

   c) Picabo Street

   d) Julia Mancuso

10. Which American basketball player is known for his "Dream Team" performance in the 1992 Barcelona Olympics?

    a) Charles Barkley

    b) Michael Jordan

    c) Kobe Bryant

    d) Shaquille O'Neal

11. Who is the American male golfer with the most Major championships?

    a) Jack Nicklaus

    b) Tiger Woods

    c) Arnold Palmer

    d) Phil Mickelson

12. Which American female swimmer won three gold medals in the 1968 Mexico City Olympics?

    a) Janet Evans

    b) Debbie Meyer

    c) Donna de Varona

    d) Missy Franklin

13. Who is the American male track and field athlete known for winning four consecutive Olympic gold medals in the same event? *Hint -discus

   a) Jim Thorpe

   b) Bob Mathias

   c) Alfred Oerter

   d) Daley Thompson

14. Which American female soccer player is known for scoring a hat trick in the 2015 FIFA Women's World Cup final?

   a) Mia Hamm

   b) Abby Wambach

   c) Carli Lloyd

   d) Brandi Chastain

15. Who is the American baseball pitcher who pitched a perfect game in the 1956 World Series?

   a) Sandy Koufax

   b) Whitey Ford

   c) Don Larsen

   d) Bob Gibson

16. Which American female figure skater is famous for landing the first triple axel in competition?

   a) Peggy Fleming

   b) Kristi Yamaguchi

   c) Tonya Harding

   d) Nancy Kerrigan

17. Who is the American football player who holds the record for the most rushing yards in a single season?

   a) Barry Sanders

   b) Emmitt Smith

   c) Eric Dickerson

   d) Walter Payton

18. Which American male tennis player is known for his 20 Grand Slam singles titles and his rivalry with Andy Roddick?

   a) Andre Agassi

   b) Pete Sampras

   c) Rafael Nadal

   d) Roger Federer

19. Who is the American female golfer who was the first woman to win the Grand Slam in a single year?

   a) Babe Zaharias

   b) Annika Sörenstam

   c) Mickey Wright

   d) Louise Suggs

20. Which New York Yankee baseball player was the first to be named both World Series MVP and All-Star MVP in the same year, 2000?

   a) Ron Guidry

   b) Don Mattingly

   c) Reggie Jackson

d) Derek Jeter

21. Who is the American male athlete known for his achievements in the sport of boxing and his iconic rivalry with Joe Frazier?

a) Muhammad Ali

b) Sugar Ray Leonard

c) George Foreman

d) Mike Tyson

22. Which American female tennis player is known for her victory in the "Battle of the Sexes" match against Bobby Riggs?

a) Serena Williams

b) Billie Jean King

c) Chris Evert

d) Martina Navratilova

23. The famous golf term "Eagle" was coined by American golfer Abe Smith at the Atlantic City Country Club in New Jersey. What does the term mean on the golf course?

a) 1 stroke under par

b) 2 strokes under par

c) 1 stroke over par

d) none of the above

24. Which American football quarterback is known for leading the New England Patriots to multiple Super Bowl victories?

a) Tom Brady

b) Peyton Manning

c) Joe Montana

d) Brett Favre

25. Who is the American female athlete known for her achievements in heptathlon and setting a world record in 1988?

   a) Jackie Joyner-Kersee

   b) Florence Griffith-Joyner

   c) Wilma Rudolph

   d) Mia Hamm

26. Which American golfer is known for his famous 18 Major championships and his nickname "The Golden Bear"?

   a) Tiger Woods

   b) Jack Nicklaus

   c) Arnold Palmer

   d) Phil Mickelson

27. What female American athlete won her first gold medal in the long jump at Paris Olympic games in 2024?

   a) Mary Decker

   b) Tara Davis-Woodhall

   c) Caster Semenya

   d) Cheryl Taplin

28. Which American basketball player is famous for his "Sky Hook" shot and winning five NBA championships with the Lakers?

   a) Wilt Chamberlain

b) Kareem Abdul-Jabbar

c) Magic Johnson

d) Jerry West

29. Who is the American female athlete known for her success in the sport of downhill skiing and winning multiple Olympic medals? She is considered one of the greatest skiers of all time, specializing in downhill and super-G.

   a) Lindsey Vonn

   b) Julia Mancuso

   c) Bode Miller

   d) Picabo Street

30. Which American male athlete is renowned for his speed in the 100m sprint and winning gold medals in the 2008 and 2012 Olympics?

   a) Carl Lewis

   b) Usain Bolt

   c) Justin Gatlin

   d) Maurice Greene

31. Who is the American female track and field athlete known for her success in the long jump and winning gold in the 1960 Rome Olympics?

   a) Wilma Rudolph

   b) Florence Griffith-Joyner

   c) Jackie Joyner-Kersee

   d) Bobbie Gibb

32. Which American baseball player is known for his career as a center fielder and his famous "Say Hey" nickname?

   a) Willie Mays

   b) Hank Aaron

   c) Babe Ruth

   d) Ty Cobb

33. What baseball team did Pete Rose play for from 1963-1978?

   a) Philadelphia Phillies

   b) New York Yankees

   c) Cincinnati Reds

   d) Boston Red Sox

34. Which American golfer is famous for his "Big Break" reality TV show and his career achievements on the PGA Tour?

   a) Phil Mickelson

   b) Tiger Woods

   c) Ben Hogan

   d) Tony Finau

35. Who is the American athlete known for his speed and success in the sport of cycling, winning the Tour de France multiple times?

   a) Lance Armstrong

   b) Greg LeMond

   c) Floyd Landis

   d) Tyler Hamilton

36. Who became the first tennis player, male or female, to win 1000 singles matches?

    a) Serena Williams

    b) John McEnroe

    c) Chris Evert

    d) Jimmy Connors

37. Who is the American male athlete who became the first to run a mile in under four minutes?

    a) Roger Bannister

    b) Jim Thorpe

    c) Jesse Owens

    d) Bill Rodgers

38. Which American figure skater is known for her "golden moment" and winning Olympic gold in 1992?

    a) Kristi Yamaguchi

    b) Tonya Harding

    c) Nancy Kerrigan

    d) Peggy Fleming

39. Who is the American female athlete known for her achievements in the sport of volleyball and winning three Olympic gold medals?

    a) Kerri Walsh Jennings

    b) Misty May-Treanor

    c) Jackie Joyner-Kersee

    d) a and b

40. Which American basketball player is known for his "Black Mamba" nickname and winning five NBA championships with the Lakers?

   a) Michael Jordan

   b) Kobe Bryant

   c) LeBron James

   d) Magic Johnson

41. Who is the American NFL quarterback who played for the Pittsburgh Steelers and had his own reality show with his family?

   a) Tom Brady

   b) Russell Wilson

   c) Terry Bradshaw

   d) Ben Roethlisberger

42. Which American baseball stadium is famous for "The Green Monster"?

   a) Camden Yards

   b) Wrigley Field

   c) Coors Field

   d) Fenway Park

43. Who is the American golfer known for his "Black Friday" victory in the 2000 U.S. Open?

   a) Tiger Woods

   b) Phil Mickelson

   c) Ben Hogan

   d) Jack Nicklaus

44. This NFL team has moved to a different city three times. From Oakland, California to Los Angeles, then back to Oakland and on to a famous city in Nevada. Can you name the team?

   a) The Chargers

   b) The Browns

   c) The Athletics

   d) The Raiders

45. This famous ice hockey game was played in the 1980 Olympic games in Lake Placid, N.Y., and played between the United States and the Soviet Union during the medal round. After the U.S. upset the Soviets 4-3, this nickname was attached to the meeting that will never be forgotten.

   a) Battle on Ice

   b) The Great Upset

   c) Miracle on Ice

   d) Game Six

46. Which American tennis player is known for his loss in the "Battle of the Sexes" match?

   a) Roger Federer

   b) Andre Agassi

   c) Bobby Riggs

   d) John McEnroe

47. Which American baseball legend is known for this famous quote, "Never let the fear of striking out get in your way"?

   a) Willie Mays

   b) Babe Ruth

   c) Mike Schmidt

d) Derek Jeter

48. Which American basketball player is famous for his innovative dunking ability from the free-throw line, multiple MVP awards, and was referred to often as "Dr. J"?

   a) Michael Jordan

   b) LeBron James

   c) Julius Erving

   d) James Harden

49. Who is the American male athlete known for his achievements in snowboarding and winning multiple gold medals at the Winter Olympics?

   a) Shaun White

   b) Tony Hawk

   c) Kelly Clark

   d) Danny Davis

50. Who was the first American woman to win an IndyCar Series race?

   a) Florence Griffith-Joyner

   b) Danica Patrick

   c) Wilma Rudolph

   d) Billie Jean King

Answers:

1. c) Muhammad Ali
2. b) Simone Biles
3. b) Michael Jordan
4. a) Michael Phelps
5. a) Serena Williams
6. b) Joe Montana
7. a) Florence Griffith-Joyner
8. c) Barry Bonds
9. b) Bode Miller
10. b) Michael Jordan
11. a) Jack Nicklaus
12. b) Debbie Meyer
13. c) Alfred Oerter
14. s) Carli Lloyd
15. c) Don Larsen
16. c) Tonya Harding
17. c) Eric Dickerson
18. d) Roger Federer
19. c) Mickey Wright
20. d) Derek Jeter
21. a) Muhammad Ali
22. b) Billie Jean King
23. b) 2 strokes under par
24. a) Tom Brady
25. a) Jackie Joyner-Kersee

26. b) Jack Nicklaus

27. b) Tara Davis-Woodhall

28. b) Kareem Abdul-Jabbar

29. a) Lindsey Vonn

30. b) Usain Bolt

31. a) Wilma Rudolph

32. a) Willie Mays

33. c) Cincinnati Reds

34. d) Tony Finau

35. a) Lance Armstrong

36. c) Chris Evert

37. a) Roger Bannister

38. a) Kristi Yamaguchi

39. d) Kerri Walsh Jennings and Misty May-Treanor

40. b) Kobe Bryant

41. c) Terry Bradshaw

42. d) Fenway Park

43. a) Tiger Woods

44. d) The Raiders

45. c) Miracle on Ice

46. c) Bobby Riggs

47. b) Babe Ruth

48. c) Julius Erving

49. a) Shaun White

50. b) Danica Patrick

Chapter 9

Do You Know the State Capitals?

1. What is the capital of California?

   a) San Francisco

   b) Sacramento

   c) Los Angeles

   d) San Diego

2. Which city is the capital of New York?

   a) New York City

   b) Albany

   c) Buffalo

   d) Syracuse

3. What is the capital of Texas?

   a) Houston

   b) Austin

   c) Dallas

   d) San Antonio

4. Which city serves as the capital of Florida?

   a) Miami

   b) Orlando

   c) Tampa

   d) Tallahassee

5. What is the capital of Illinois?

   a) Chicago

b) Springfield

c) Peoria

d) Naperville

6. Which city is the capital of Washington state?

   a) Seattle

   b) Tacoma

   c) Spokane

   d) Olympia

7. What is the capital of Colorado?

   a) Denver

   b) Colorado Springs

   c) Boulder

   d) Aurora

8. Which city is the capital of Georgia?

   a) Atlanta

   b) Savannah

   c) Augusta

   d) Macon

9. What is the capital of Ohio?

   a) Cleveland

   b) Columbus

   c) Cincinnati

d) Toledo

10. Which city is the capital of Michigan?

   a) Detroit

   b) Lansing

   c) Grand Rapids

   d) Flint

11. What is the capital of Pennsylvania?

   a) Philadelphia

   b) Pittsburgh

   c) Harrisburg

   d) Allentown

12. Which city serves as the capital of Arizona?

   a) Phoenix

   b) Tucson

   c) Mesa

   d) Scottsdale

13. What is the capital of Massachusetts?

   a) Boston

   b) Worcester

   c) Springfield

   d) Cambridge

14. Which city is the capital of Tennessee?

   a) Memphis

   b) Nashville

   c) Knoxville

   d) Chattanooga

15. What is the capital of North Carolina?

   a) Charlotte

   b) Raleigh

   c) Greensboro

   d) Durham

16. Which city serves as the capital of South Carolina?

   a) Charleston

   b) Greenville

   c) Columbia

   d) Spartanburg

17. What is the capital of Nevada?

   a) Reno

   b) Las Vegas

   c) Carson City

   d) Henderson

18. Which city is the capital of Oregon?

   a) Portland

b) Eugene

c) Salem

d) Bend

19. What is the capital of Indiana?

   a) Indianapolis

   b) Fort Wayne

   c) Evansville

   d) South Bend

20. Which city is the capital of New Jersey?

   a) Newark

   b) Trenton

   c) Camden

   d) Hoboken

21. What is the capital of Kentucky?

   a) Louisville

   b) Lexington

   c) Frankfort

   d) Bowling Green

22. Which city serves as the capital of Maine?

   a) Portland

   b) Bangor

   c) Augusta

d) Lewiston

23. What is the capital of Maryland?

   a) Baltimore

   b) Annapolis

   c) Silver Spring

   d) Frederick

24. Which city is the capital of Alabama?

   a) Birmingham

   b) Mobile

   c) Montgomery

   d) Huntsville

25. What is the capital of West Virginia?

   a) Charleston

   b) Huntington

   c) Morgantown

   d) Wheeling

26. Which city serves as the capital of Mississippi?

   a) Jackson

   b) Biloxi

   c) Gulfport

   d) Hattiesburg

27. What is the capital of Wisconsin?

   a) Milwaukee

   b) Madison

   c) Green Bay

   d) Kenosha

28. Which city is the capital of Iowa?

   a) Des Moines

   b) Cedar Rapids

   c) Davenport

   d) Sioux City

29. What is the capital of Nebraska?

   a) Omaha

   b) Lincoln

   c) Grand Island

   d) Bellevue

30. Which city serves as the capital of Arkansas?

   a) Little Rock

   b) Fayetteville

   c) Hot Springs

   d) Fort Smith

31. What is the capital of Kansas?

   a) Wichita

b) Topeka

c) Lawrence

d) Overland Park

32. Which city is the capital of South Dakota?

    a) Sioux Falls

    b) Rapid City

    c) Pierre

    d) Aberdeen

33. What is the capital of North Dakota?

    a) Fargo

    b) Bismarck

    c) Grand Forks

    d) Minot

34. Which city serves as the capital of Montana?

    a) Billings

    b) Great Falls

    c) Helena

    d) Missoula

35. What is the capital of Idaho?

    a) Boise

    b) Idaho Falls

    c) Twin Falls

d) Pocatello

36. Which city is the capital of Wyoming?

   a) Casper

   b) Cheyenne

   c) Laramie

   d) Gillette

37. What is the capital of Alaska?

   a) Anchorage

   b) Fairbanks

   c) Juneau

   d) Sitka

38. Which city serves as the capital of Hawaii?

   a) Honolulu

   b) Hilo

   c) Kailua

   d) Maui

39. What is the capital of Utah?

   a) Salt Lake City

   b) Provo

   c) Ogden

   d) St. George

40. Which city is the capital of New Mexico?

    a) Albuquerque

    b) Santa Fe

    c) Las Cruces

    d) Roswell

41. What is the capital of Oklahoma?

    a) Tulsa

    b) Norman

    c) Oklahoma City

    d) Edmond

42. Which city serves as the capital of Delaware?

    a) Wilmington

    b) Dover

    c) Newark

    d) Georgetown

43. What is the capital of Rhode Island?

    a) Providence

    b) Newport

    c) Warwick

    d) Cranston

44. Which city is the capital of Connecticut?

    a) Hartford

b) New Haven

c) Bridgeport

d) Stamford

45. What is the capital of Louisiana?

a) New Orleans

b) Lafayette

c) Shreveport

d) Baton Rouge

46. Which city serves as the capital of Missouri?

a) Jefferson City

b) Kansas City

c) Colombia

d) St. Louis

47. What is the capital of Minnesota?

a) Saint Paul

b) Grand Rapids

c) Grand Forks

d) Alexandria

48. Which city is the capital of Vermont?

a) Burlington

b) Montpelier

c) Rutland

d) Stowe

49. What is the capital of New Hampshire?

a) Concord

b) Manchester

c) Nashua

d) Portsmouth

50. Which city serves as the capital of Virginia?

a) Richmond

b) Williamsburg

c) Arlington

d) Chincoteague

Answers:

1. b) Sacramento

2. b) Albany

3. b) Austin

4. d) Tallahassee

5. b) Springfield

6. d) Olympia

7. a) Denver

8. a) Atlanta

9. b) Columbus

10. b) Lansing

11. c) Harrisburg

12. a) Phoenix

13. a) Boston

14. b) Nashville

15. b) Raleigh

16. c) Columbia

17. c) Carson City

18. c) Salem

19. a) Indianapolis

20. b) Trenton

21. c) Frankfort

22. c) Augusta

23. b) Annapolis

24. c) Montgomery

25. a) Charleston

26. a) Jackson

27. b) Madison

28. a) Des Moines

29. b) Lincoln

30. a) Little Rock

31. b) Topeka

32. c) Pierre

33. b) Bismarck

34. c) Helena

35. a) Boise

36. b) Cheyenne

37. c) Juneau

38. a) Honolulu

39. a) Salt Lake City

40. b) Santa Fe

41. c) Oklahoma City

42. b) Dover

43. a) Providence

44. a) Hartford

45. d) Baton Rouge

46. a) Jefferson City

47. a) Saint Paul

48. b) Montpelier

49. a) Concord

50. a) Richmond

Chapter 10

Fun Facts About Our State Capitals

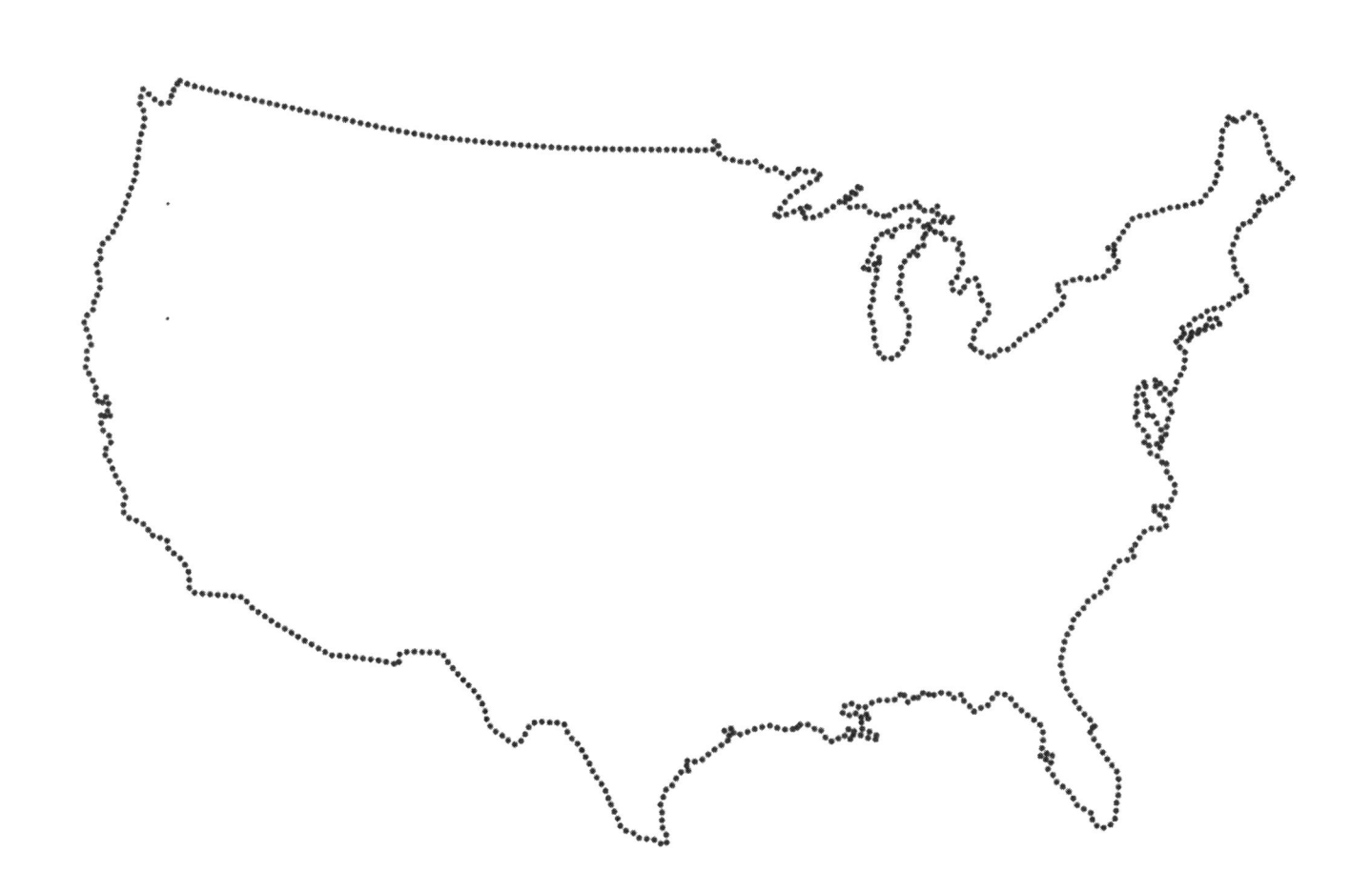

1. Which capital city is known for being the highest elevation state capital in the U.S.? This city is rich in Native American heritage, is considered one of the most romantic cities in the country and has a famed Margarita Trail.

   a) Denver, Colorado

   b) Santa Fe, New Mexico

   c) Salt Lake City, Utah

   d) Carson City, Nevada

2. This northern state capital is known as a platinum-rated biking city with many parks and glacial waterways. This city is known for its craft beverages and cheese.

   a) Albany, New York

   b) Cheyenne, Wyoming

   c) St. Paul, Minnesota

   d) Madison, Wisconsin

3. Originally an English trading post on the Kennebec River, this capital city is known for outdoor activities including hiking in the Vaughan Woods State Park. This city is known for its family friendly atmosphere.

   a) Little Rock, Arkansas

   b) Olympia, Washington

   c) Helena, Montana

   d) Augusta, Maine

4. Which capital city is known for its Gold Rush which was a pivotal event that transformed this city into a thriving commercial and supply hub for gold miners? This city is known as "City of Trees" which refers to its abundant urban forest. This city has more trees per capita than any other city in the world.

   a) Sacramento, California

b) San Francisco, California

c) Los Angeles, California

d) San Diego, California

5. Which state capital is named after a U.S. President?

a) Jackson, Mississippi

b) Lincoln, Nebraska

c) Madison, Wisconsin

d) All of the above

6. Which U.S. capital city is known for its famous annual "Mardi Gras" celebration? This city has been the filming location for many movies, including Captain Marvel, Twilight: Breaking Dawn, and Interview with a Vampire. It is known as "The Red Stick City".

a) Baton Rouge, Louisiana

b) Montgomery, Alabama

c) New Orleans, Louisiana

d) Jackson, Mississippi

7. Which capital city is located on the island of Oahu and is known for its Pearl Harbor memorial?

a) Hilo, Hawaii

b) Honolulu, Hawaii

c) Kailua, Hawaii

d) Maui, Hawaii

8. This U.S. capital in known for their Frontier Days which boast the world's largest outdoor rodeo and Western festival. This city is also known for Big Boots which can be found all over this city, especially downtown, and each boot tells a story.

   a) Cheyenne, Wyoming

   b) Olympia, Washington

   c) Boise, Idaho

   d) Carson City, Nevada

9. In 2015, this capital city was voted to be the "Boardwalk" city in the updated version of the Monopoly board game, "Monopoly Here & Now" edition. This city replaced Atlantic City, New Jersey as the location of the Boardwalk.

   a) Charleston, West Virginia

   b) Sacramento, California

   c) Pierre, South Dakota

   d) Montgomery, Alabama

10. Which U.S. capital is known for having the oldest state capital and the oldest public building in the country?

    a) Austin, Texas

    b) Denver, Colorado

    c) Boston, Massachusetts

    d) Santa Fe, New Mexico

11. This state capital is home to a state university whose football team plays on a blue field. It is considered one of the best mid-size cities in the U.S. for it low cost of living. The river named for this city flows over 100 miles from the Rocky Mountains to the Snake River.

    a) Portland, Oregon

    b) Denver, Colorado

c) Phoenix, Arizona

d) Boise, Idaho

12. Which U.S. capital city is home to one of the largest and top zoos and aquariums in the world with over 10,000 animals and 580 acres of land? This city boasts the first Junior High School in the United States and is still in operation today. The famed golfer Jack Nicklaus was born in this city in 1940.

   a) Columbus, Ohio

   b) Philadelphia, Pennsylvania

   c) Boston, Massachusetts

   d) Richmond, Virginia

13. Which state capital is known for its picturesque location along the Willamette River?

   a) Salem, Oregon

   b) Boise, Idaho

   c) Olympia, Washington

   d) Helena, Montana

14. Which U.S. capital is famous for its vibrant arts scene and annual Sundance Film Festival?

   a) Denver, Colorado

   b) Salt Lake City, Utah

   c) Austin, Texas

   d) Nashville, Tennessee

15. Which capital city is known for being the home to many famous bourbon distilleries (Angle's Envy and Coppers & Kings) and bourbon themed accommodations, shopping and culinary trails?

a) Nashville, Tennessee

b) Louisville, Kentucky

c) Charleston, West Virginia

d) Denver, Colorado

16. Which New England U.S. capital city is known for its beautiful and historic "Old North Church," a site of the American Revolution? The cookie, Fig Newton, was named after a suburb in this city.

a) Boston, Massachusetts

b) Philadelphia, Pennsylvania

c) New York City, New York

d) Concord, New Hampshire

17. Which U.S. capital city is known as the Live Music Capital of the World? This city is the birthplace of some famous folks such as Glen Powell, Tom Ford, Ethan Hawke, and Dabney Coleman.

a) Austin, Texas

b) Nashville, Tennessee

c) Salt Lake City, Utah

d) Phoenix, Arizona

18. Which U.S. capital city is famous for hosting one of the largest "First Friday" art walks in the country? This city is also known for being home to the Edgar Allan Poe Museum. Also, it can be argued that the First Thanksgiving was celebrated in this city in 1619.

a) Phoenix, Arizona

b) Las Vegas, Nevada

c) Santa Fe, New Mexico

d) Richmond, Virginia

19. Which state capital is renowned for its annual "Celtic Fest" celebrating Scottish and Irish heritage?

　a) Denver, Colorado

　b) Salem, Oregon

　c) Boston, Massachusetts

　d) Nashville, Tennessee

20. This US capital city is famous for being the birthplace of Abraham Lincoln. It has been known as the "City of Firsts", which was earned through a history of innovation, including America's first Armory and military arsenal and the first American automobile, and the birthplace of basketball.

　a) Montgomery, Alabama

　b) Springfield, Illinois

　c) Charleston, West Virginia

　d) Jackson, Mississippi

21. Which capital city is known for its Mediterranean climate with mild winters and warm summers, and average temperatures of 61 degrees F?

　a) Sacramento, California

　b) San Francisco, California

　c) Los Angeles, California

　d) San Diego, California

22. Which U.S. capital city is located at the base of the Olympic Peninsula and is a popular destination for travelers on their way to the ocean? It is close to Mt. Rainier National Park and the Puget Sound.

　a) Olympia, Washington

b) Portland, Oregon

c) Denver, Colorado

d) San Francisco, California

23. This state capital is known for being the smallest state capital in the United States, and for its historic charm. Also, the Winooski River runs through this city.

   a) Louisville, Kentucky

   b) Nashville, Tennessee

   c) Charleston, West Virginia

   d) Montpelier, Vermont

24. This capital city played a role in the ratification of the Declaration of Independence and is known for an International Speedway which is the largest concrete-only NASCAR racing venue in the world.

   a) Providence, Rhode Island

   b) Boston, Massachusetts

   c) Hartford, Connecticut

   d) Dover, Delaware

25. Which state capital is recognized for its "Mormon Tabernacle Choir" and historic temple?

   a) Salt Lake City, Utah

   b) Boise, Idaho

   c) Denver, Colorado

   d) Austin, Texas

26. Which northern U.S. capital city is known for its "Woodstock" festival site?

a) Albany, New York

b) Philadelphia, Pennsylvania

c) Boston, Massachusetts

d) Washington, D.C.

27. This capital city is famous for its location between Yellowstone and Glacier National Parks and is known as the birthplace of disc golf and has more courses than any other place around its state.

a) Little Rock, Arkansas

b) Helena, Montana

c) Boise, Idaho

d) Providence, Rhode Island

28. This capital city is the birthplace of Oldsmobile: The Olds Motor Vehicle Company was founded in 1897.

a) Lansing, Michigan

b) Philadelphia, Pennsylvania

c) Boston, Massachusetts

d) New York City, New York

29. Which state capital is famous for its "Blue Ridge Mountains" views and historic architecture? This city is the home to Shaw University and Marbles Kids Museum, a nationally renowned museum with interactive exhibits for kids.

a) Raleigh, North Carolina

b) Charleston, West Virginia

c) Montgomery, Alabama

d) Nashville, Tennessee

30. This capital city is only accessible by air or water because of the rugged terrain around the city. The city was founded by gold miners in 1880. The downtown area is so compact that you can see it all without a rental car.

   a) Lincoln, Nebraska

   b) Providence, Rhode Island

   c) St. Paul, Minnesota

   d) Juneau, Alaska

31. This southern capital is known for its iconic music and African American heritage. Known for delighting in soul food classics, Southern fusion, Gulf seafood, tamales, Cajun, and more. This city was named for a U.S. president and established in 1821. This city is also considered the birthplace of Blues.

   a) Nashville, Tennessee

   b) Jackson, Mississippi

   c) Montgomery, Alabama

   d) Phoenix, Arizona

32. This state capital is the home to a world-famous speedway and is known as the racing capital of the world. They also have a football team where the famed Peyton Manning and Reggie Wayne played.

   a) Nashville, Tennessee

   b) Indianapolis, Indiana

   c) Washington, D.C.

   d) Seattle, Washington

33. Which Pacific Northwest state capital is celebrated as the "Cherry City" because of its history of cherry cultivation and production? This city hosts an annual Cherry Festival.

a) Salem, Oregon

b) Boise, Idaho

c) Denver, Colorado

d) Olympia, Washington

34. Which U.S. capital city is known for its significant "Civil Rights Movement" history and museums? Martin Luther King, Jr. preached at the Dexter Avenue Baptist Church in this city.

a) Montgomery, Alabama

b) Jackson, Mississippi

c) Atlanta, Georgia

d) Nashville, Tennessee

35. Which state capital was the fourth largest city in colonial America and the wealthiest? The first golf club in America was established in this city in 1787.

a) Concord, New Hampshire

b) Boston, Massachusetts

c) Providence, Rhode Island

d) Charleston, West Virginia

36. Which U.S. capital city is known for its vibrant "Music Row" and country music scene?

a) Austin, Texas

b) Nashville, Tennessee

c) Memphis, Tennessee

d) Louisville, Kentucky

37. Which state capital's name is said to mean "a good place to dig potatoes"? This city has a strong connection to the Civil Rights Movement, home of the Evel Knievel Museum, and Washburn University.

   a) Jackson, Mississippi

   b) Charleston, West Virginia

   c) Topeka, Kansas

   d) Raleigh, North Carolina

38. There is a famous bridge in this capital city which is better known as… "_____Makes the World Takes Bridge". This is illuminated on two of the bridge's steel trusses. Fill in the blank with this capital city.

   a) Harrisburg, Pennsylvania

   b) San Francisco, California

   c) Baton Rouge, Louisianna

   d) Trenton, New Jersey

39. Which state capital is celebrated for its "Desert Botanical Garden" and unique flora?

   a) Phoenix, Arizona

   b) Las Vegas, Nevada

   c) Santa Fe, New Mexico

   d) Boise, Idaho

40. This U.S. capital city is not as well-known as its world-famous sister city 3 hours away, but this capital is pretty wonderful too. It was home to Martin Van Buren, the College of Saint Rose, and known for its famous fish fry sandwich. This city is the birthplace of the telegraph, electric motor, celluloid plastic, dominos, and perforated toilet paper.

   a) Albany, New York

   b) Harrisburg, Pennsylvania

c) Columbia, South Carolina

d) Tallahassee, Florida

41. Which state capital is recognized for its Clinton Presidential Center, Little Rock Nine, and the ESSE Purse Museum?

a) Santa Fe, New Mexico

b) Denver, Colorado

c) Little Rock, Arkansas

d) Portland, Oregon

42. This state capital boasts the invention of the First American alarm clock. It is located near the Merrimack River. America's beloved hero Christa McAuliffe taught at this city's high school.

a) Concord, New Hampshire

b) Boston, Massachusetts

c) Harrisburg, Pennsylvania

d) Richmond, Virginia

43. Which state capital is located on the bluffs of the Missouri River and in a major wine-producing region? This city is also close to the Lewis and Clark National Historic Trail.

a) Pierre, South Dakota

b) Helena, Montana

c) Jefferson City, Missouri

d) Montpelier, Vermont

44. Which U.S. capital city is known as the Insurance Capital of the World? It holds the Mark Twain House and Museum, the Harriet Beecher Stowe Center and Lorelai Gilmore's parents lived there.

a) Boston, Massachusetts

b) Providence, Rhode Island

c) Hartford, Connecticut

d) Richmond, Virginia

45. Which state capital is famous for its "National Cowboy & Western Heritage Museum"? This city is also home to one of the world's largest livestock markets.

a) Oklahoma City, Oklahoma

b) Denver, Colorado

c) Austin, Texas

d) Nashville, Tennessee

46. This southern U.S. capital city is known as the "hilliest" spot in its state. It has the third tallest capital building in the U.S. Its name comes from a Muskogean Indian word that means "Old Fields" and is also known for its rolling red hills.

a) Montgomery, Alabama

b) Baton Rouge, Louisiana

c) Charleston, West Virginia

d) Tallahassee, Florida

47. Which state capital is celebrated for its "Gilded Age" architecture and historic homes? This city is the home of Brown University.

a) Providence, Rhode Island

b) Nashville, Tennessee

c) Charleston, South Carolina

d) Boston, Massachusetts

48. Which U.S. capital city was the scene of the National Tariff Convention of 1827, is located on the Susquehanna River and is the birthplace of the polarizing figure in American politics, Mr. Newt Gingrich?

   a) Charleston, South Carolina

   b) Harrisburg, Pennsylvania

   c) New Orleans, Louisiana

   d) Mobile, Alabama

49. This capital city is best known as the "Mile High City" because elevation-wise, it is a mile high. This city is close to the Rocky Mountains, and hosts five major professional sports teams.

   a) Boise, Idaho

   b) Denver, Colorado

   c) Helena, Montana

   d) Salt Lake City, Utah

50. This capital forms the "Twin Cities" with its neighboring famous city. This city is known for its cold, snowy winters and humid summers. This city is the birthplace of the famed author F. Scott Fitzgerald, Olympic skier Lindsay Vonn, and actor Josh Harnett.

   a) Cheyenne, Wyoming

   b) Denver, Colorado

   c) St. Paul, Minnesota

   d) Madison, Wisconsin

Answers:

1. b) Santa Fe, New Mexico

2. d) Madison, Wisconsin

3. d) Augusta, Maine

4. a) Sacramento, California

5. d) All of the above

6. a) Baton Rouge, Louisiana

7. b) Honolulu, Hawaii

8. a) Cheyenne, Wyoming

9. c) Pierre, South Dakota

10. d) Santa Fe, New Mexico

11. d) Boise, Idaho

12. a) Columbus, Ohio

13. a) Salem, Oregon

14. b) Salt Lake City, Utah

15. b) Louisville, Kentucky

16. a) Boston, Massachusetts

17. a) Austin, Texas

18. d) Richmond, Virginia

19. c) Boston, Massachusetts

20. b) Springfield, Illinois

21. a) Sacramento, California

22. a) Olympia, Washington

23. d) Montpelier, Vermont

24. d) Dover, Delaware

25. a) Salt Lake City, Utah

26. a) Albany, New York

27. b) Helena, Montana

28. a) Lansing, Michigan

29. a) Raleigh, North Carolina

30. d) Juneau, Alaska

31. a) Jackson, Mississippi

32. b) Indianapolis, Indiana

33. a) Salem, Oregon

34. a) Montgomery, Alabama

35. d) Charleston, West Virginia

36. b) Nashville, Tennessee

37. c) Topeka, Kansas

38. d) Trenton, New Jersey

39. a) Phoenix, Arizona

40. a) Albany, New York

41. c) Little Rock, Arkansas

42. a) Concord, New Hampshire

43. c) Jefferson City, Missouri

44. c) Hartford, Connecticut

45. a) Oklahoma City, Oklahoma

46. d) Tallahassee, Florida

47. a) Providence, Rhode Island

48. b) Harrisburg, Pennsylvania

49. b) Denver, Colorado

50. c) St. Paul, Minnesota

Chapter 11

Legendary American Sporting Events

1. Which NFL team famously made a comeback from a 28-3 deficit to win Super Bowl LI?

   a) Atlanta Falcons

   b) New England Patriots

   c) Seattle Seahawks

   d) Green Bay Packers

2. Which NBA team broke the single season win record with 73 wins in the 2015-2016 season?

   a) Cleveland Cavaliers

   b) Golden State Warriors

   c) Chicago Bulls

   d) Miami Heat

3. Which NHL team won the Stanley Cup in 2019 after a 49-year championship drought?

   a) Chicago Blackhawks

   b) Boston Bruins

   c) St. Louis Blues

   d) Detroit Red Wings

4. Who is the golfer known for his dramatic victory at the 1997 Masters, where he won by 12 strokes?

   a) Phil Mickelson

   b) Rory McIlroy

   c) Tiger Woods

   d) Jack Nicklaus

5. Which WNBA team won the championship in 2008 with a decisive 3-0 series victory?

a) Seattle Storm

   b) Detroit Shock

   c) Los Angeles Sparks

   d) Minnesota Lynx

6. Which MLB player hit a walk-off home run in Game 6 of the 1993 World Series, clinching the title for his team?

   a) Ken Griffey Jr.

   b) Joe Carter

   c) Barry Bonds

   d) Mark McGwire

7. Which NASCAR driver is known for his dramatic "Daytona 500" win in 2001, just after the death of his father, Dale Earnhardt Sr.?

   a) Jeff Gordon

   b) Dale Earnhardt Jr.

   c) Jimmie Johnson

   d) Tony Stewart

8. Which NFL player famously guaranteed a Super Bowl victory and delivered with a win in Super Bowl III?

   a) Joe Namath

   b) Johnny Unitas

   c) Terry Bradshaw

   d) Tom Brady

9. Which NBA player scored 100 points in a single game in 1962, a record that still stands?

a) Michael Jordan

b) Wilt Chamberlain

c) Kobe Bryant

d) LeBron James

10. Which NHL event is known for its dramatic and controversial "Bobby Orr Goal" in the 1970 Stanley Cup Finals?

a) The "Miracle on Ice"

b) The "Broad Street Bullies"

c) Bobby Orr's Flying Goal

d) The "Fog Bowl"

11. Which PGA golfer famously made an incredible comeback to win the 2019 Masters after not winning a major for over a decade?

a) Phil Mickelson

b) Rory McIlroy

c) Tiger Woods

d) Brooks Koepka

12. This Power Forward WNBA player plays for the New York Liberty and was born in Syracuse, New York.

a) Diana Taurasi

b) Tamika Catchings

c) Liz Cambage

d) Breanna Stewart

13. Which MLB team ended an 86-year World Series drought with a victory in 2004?

a) Chicago Cubs

b) Boston Red Sox

c) New York Yankees

d) Los Angeles Dodgers

14. Which NASCAR race is famously known as the "Great American Race"?

a) The Brickyard 400

b) The Southern 500

c) The Daytona 500

d) The Coca-Cola 600

15. Which NFL team won Super Bowl XLVIII with a dominant 43-8 victory over the Denver Broncos?

a) Seattle Seahawks

b) New England Patriots

c) San Francisco 49ers

d) Pittsburgh Steelers

16. Which NBA Finals series was famously decided by Ray Allen's clutch three-pointer in Game 6 of the 2013 Finals?

a) Miami Heat vs. San Antonio Spurs

b) Golden State Warriors vs. Cleveland Cavaliers

c) Boston Celtics vs. Los Angeles Lakers

d) Chicago Bulls vs. Utah Jazz

17. Which amateur team was known for its "Miracle on Ice" victory over the Soviet Union in the 1980 Winter Olympics?

a) Canada

  b) Sweden

  c) Finland

  d) USA

18. Which PGA golfer won the U.S. Open in 2018 with a dramatic final-round comeback?

    a) Tiger Woods

    b) Brooks Koepka

    c) Phil Mickelson

    d) Justin Rose

19. Which WNBA team won the most championships in the 2010s?

    a) Minnesota Lynx

    b) Los Angeles Sparks

    c) Seattle Storm

    d) Phoenix Mercury

20. Which MLB player famously broke the single-season home run record in 2001, surpassing Mark McGwire?

    a) Sammy Sosa

    b) Barry Bonds

    c) Ken Griffey Jr.

    d) Alex Rodriguez

21. Which NASCAR driver is known for winning the 2004 NASCAR Cup Series Championship in dramatic fashion with a last-lap pass?

    a) Kurt Busch

b) Jeff Gordon

c) Jimmie Johnson

d) Tony Stewart

22. Which NFL game is remembered for the "Immaculate Reception" by Franco Harris in 1972?

a) Pittsburgh Steelers vs. Oakland Raiders

b) Dallas Cowboys vs. Miami Dolphins

c) New England Patriots vs. St. Louis Rams

d) San Francisco 49ers vs. Cincinnati Bengals

23. Which NBA team won the 2000 Finals with an iconic game-winning shot by Shaquille O'Neal and Kobe Bryant?

a) Los Angeles Lakers

b) Indiana Pacers

c) Chicago Bulls

d) New York Knicks

24. Which NHL player scored the game-winning goal in the "Summit Series" against the Soviet Union in 1972?

a) Bobby Orr

b) Paul Henderson

c) Wayne Gretzky

d) Mario Lemieux

25. Which PGA golfer famously won the 2012 PGA Championship by a record-setting margin of eight strokes?

a) Rory McIlroy

b) Jason Day

c) Phil Mickelson

d) Jordan Spieth

26. Which WNBA player set the record for most career points scored in the league?

a) Tamika Catchings

b) Diana Taurasi

c) Maya Moore

d) Sue Bird

27. Which MLB team's "Billy Goat Curse" was famously broken with a World Series win in 2016?

a) Chicago Cubs

b) Boston Red Sox

c) New York Mets

d) Chicago White Sox

28. Which NASCAR event is known for being the final race of the NASCAR Cup Series season?

a) Daytona 500

b) Coca-Cola 600

c) Southern 500

d) NASCAR Cup Series Championship Race

29. Which NFL team is known for its historic "Greatest Show on Turf" offense in the early 2000s?

a) St. Louis Rams

b) New England Patriots

c) Indianapolis Colts

d) San Diego Chargers

30. Which NBA player achieved a quadruple-double in 1979, becoming the first player to do so?

a) Wilt Chamberlain

b) Magic Johnson

c) Nate Thurmond

d) Julius Erving

31. Which NHL team was known for the "Broad Street Bullies" nickname during their dominant era in the 1970s?

a) Philadelphia Flyers

b) New York Rangers

c) Montreal Canadiens

d) Boston Bruins

32. The greatest comeback in U.S. Open history led to the greatest visor toss in U.S. Open history. Name that golfer.

a) Phil Mickelson

b) Tiger Woods

c) Rory McIlroy

d) Arnold Palmer

33. Which WNBA team won four championships in a row?

a) Minnesota Lynx

b) Houston Comets

c) Seattle Storm

d) Washington Mystics

34. Which MLB player famously hit a home run during the "Shot Heard 'Round the World" game in 1951?

a) Bobby Thomson

b) Babe Ruth

c) Hank Aaron

d) Mickey Mantle

35. Which NASCAR driver was known for his "Number 3" car and tragic death in a crash at the 2001 Daytona 500?

a) Dale Earnhardt Sr.

b) Richard Petty

c) Jeff Gordon

d) Rusty Wallace

36. Which NFL game is remembered for the "Music City Miracle," where the Tennessee Titans pulled off a dramatic last-second play?

a) Titans vs. Buffalo Bills

b) Patriots vs. Rams

c) Steelers vs. Cowboys

d) Packers vs. Giants

37. Which NBA player famously scored 81 points in a single game in 2006, the second-highest single-game score in NBA history?

   a) Kobe Bryant

   b) Michael Jordan

   c) Wilt Chamberlain

   d) LeBron James

38. Which NHL player scored the most goals in a single season, setting a record in 1981?

   a) Wayne Gretzky

   b) Mario Lemieux

   c) Brett Hull

   d) Alexander Ovechkin

39. Which PGA tournament is known for its famous "Green Jacket" awarded to the winner?

   a) The Open Championship

   b) The U.S. Open

   c) The Masters Tournament

   d) The PGA Championship

40. Which WNBA player is famous for hitting the game-winning shot in the 2009 WNBA Finals?

   a) Diana Taurasi

   b) Ebony Hoffman

   c) Lauren Jackson

   d) Sue Bird

41. Which MLB team won the 2016 World Series with a historic comeback from a 3-1 deficit?

   a) Chicago Cubs

   b) Cleveland Indians

   c) New York Mets

   d) San Francisco Giants

42. Which NASCAR driver won the 2015 NASCAR Cup Series Championship with a dramatic final race victory?

   a) Kyle Busch

   b) Kevin Harvick

   c) Jimmie Johnson

   d) Joey Logano

43. Which NFL player famously returned a kickoff 108 yards for a touchdown in the Super Bowl?

   a) Devin Hester

   b) James Harrison

   c) Marcus Allen

   d) Jacoby Jones

44. Which NBA team is known for its "Bad Boys" era during the late 1980s and early 1990s?

   a) Detroit Pistons

   b) Chicago Bulls

   c) Boston Celtics

   d) Los Angeles Lakers

45. In March 1994, Wayne Gretzky make hockey history scoring his 802nd goal in a historic game against the Vancouver Canucks. What team was he playing for?

   a) Edmonton Oilers

   b) Buffalo Sabres

   c) Montreal Canadiens

   d) Los Angeles Kings

46. Which PGA golfer famously won the 2008 U.S. Open after playing 91 holes due to a playoff?

   a) Tiger Woods

   b) Phil Mickelson

   c) Rocco Mediate

   d) Sergio Garcia

47. Game 6 of the 1986 World Series between the New York Mets and the Boston Red Sox is considered one of the most famous games in baseball history. The Mets won the game off an error by Red Sox first baseman _____?

   a) Mookie Wilson

   b) Gary Carter

   c) Bill Buckner

   d) Babe Ruth

48. The MLB pitcher, Mariano Rivera, is known as the undisputed king of the closer's, which earned him what moniker?

   a) The Babe

   b) The Captain

   c) The Big Hurt

d) The Sandman

49. The 1979 Daytona 500 is said to have put NASCAR on the map, and is known for the famous words, "AND THERE'S A FIGHT". Who won that race?

    a) Cale Yarborough

    b) Jeff Gordon

    c) Richard Petty

    d) Bill Elliott

50. The 1958 NFL Championship captured the attention of the nation and is considered "The Greatest Game Ever Played". The Baltimore Colts defeated what team 23-17.

    a) New York Giants

    b) Oakland Raiders

    c) Dallas Cowboys

    d) Green Bay Packers

Answers:

1. b) New England Patriots

2. b) Golden State Warriors

3. c) St. Louis Blues

4. c) Tiger Woods

5. b) Detroit Shock

6. b) Joe Carter

7. b) Dale Earnhardt Jr.

8. a) Joe Namath

9. b) Wilt Chamberlain

10. c) Bobby Orr's Flying Goal

11. c) Tiger Woods

12. d) Breanna Stewart

13. b) Boston Red Sox

14. c) The Daytona 500

15. a) Seattle Seahawks

16. a) Miami Heat vs. San Antonio Spurs

17. d) USA

18. b) Brooks Koepka

19. a) Minnesota Lynx

20. b) Barry Bonds

21. a) Kurt Busch

22. a) Pittsburgh Steelers vs. Oakland Raiders

23. a) Los Angeles Lakers

24. b) Paul Henderson

25. a) Rory McIlroy

26. b) Diana Taurasi

27. a) Chicago Cubs

28. d) NASCAR Cup Series Championship Race

29. a) St. Louis Rams

30. c) Nate Thurmond

31. a) Philadelphia Flyers

32. d) Arnold Palmer

33. b) Houston Comets

34. a) Bobby Thomson

35. a) Dale Earnhardt Sr.

36. a) Titans vs. Buffalo Bills

37. a) Kobe Bryant

38. a) Wayne Gretzky

39. c) The Masters Tournament

40. b) Ebony Hoffman

41. a) Chicago Cubs

42. a) Kyle Busch

43. d) Jacoby Jones

44. a) Detroit Pistons

45. d) Los Angeles Kings

46. a) Tiger Woods

47. c) Bill Buckner

48. d) The Sandman

49. c) Richard Petty

50. a) New York Giants

Chapter 12

<u>American Television</u>

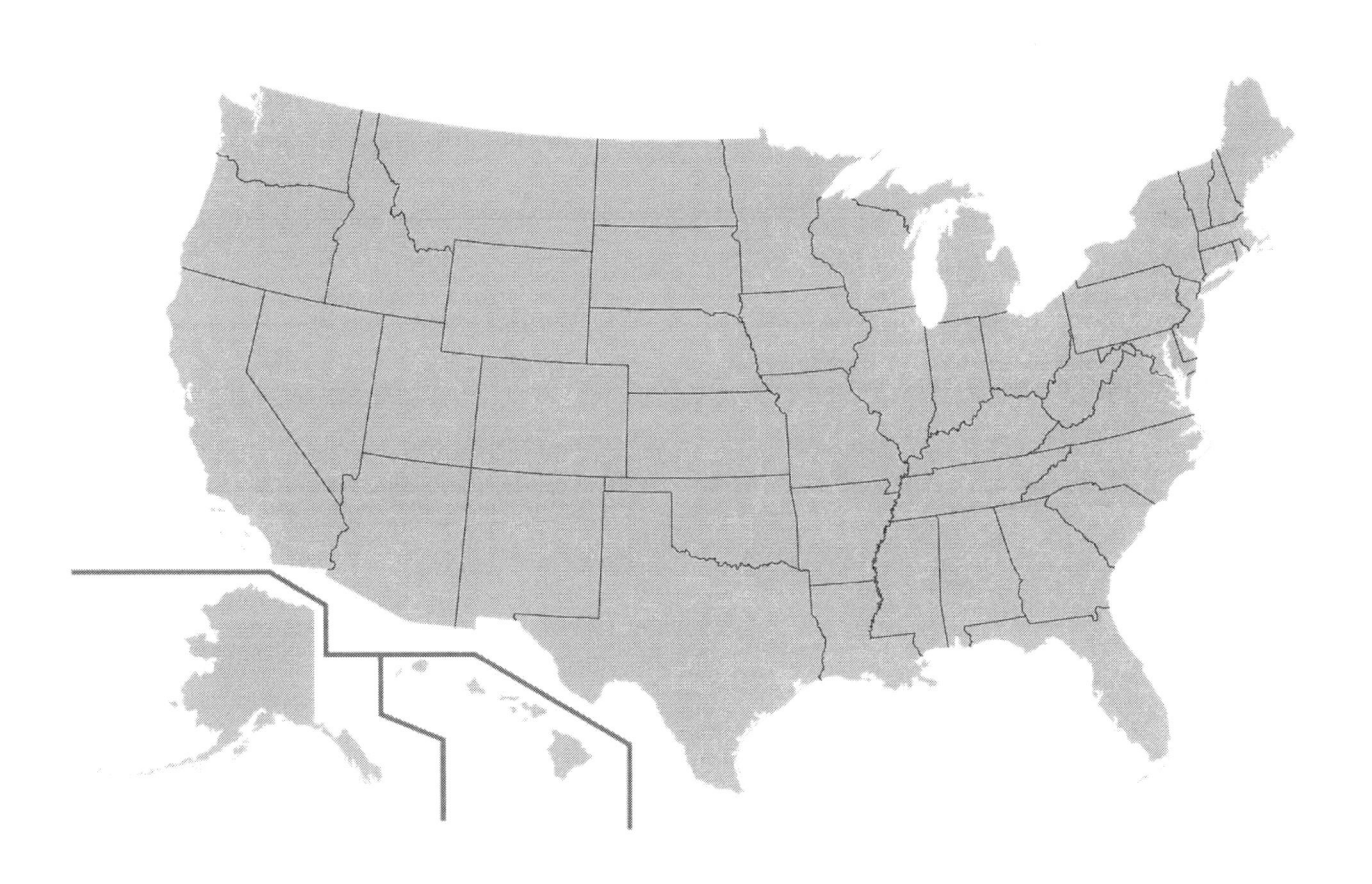

1. This popular drama follows a financial planner, Marty Byrde, who relocates his family from Chicago to a summer resort community to continue his work money laundering.

   a) Better Call Saul

   b) Breaking Bad

   c) Narcos

   d) Ozark

2. What popular Netflix series follows the lead character "John B" and his three best friends hunting for a treasure linked to his father's disappearance?

   a) Sweet Home Alabama

   b) Outer Banks

   c) Daredevil

   d) How I Met Your Mother

3. Which TV show, set in the late 1970s, revolves around a wealthy mystery man who runs a detective agency where three savvy, smart and gorgeous women are the detectives who always save the day?

   a) Three's Company

   b) The Bob Newhart Show

   c) Rhoda

   d) Charlie's Angels

4. Which TV show, created by Shonda Rhimes, follows the life of a crisis management expert working for the President of the United States?

   a) Grey's Anatomy

   b) Scandal

   c) How to Get Away with Murder

d) Private Practice

5. In which TV series does the character Sheldon Cooper work at Caltech and is known for his eccentric behavior?

   a) The Big Bang Theory

   b) How I Met Your Mother

   c) Community

   d) Parks and Recreation

6. Which TV show centers around a suburban family where the father has a successful career in the television industry?

   a) Home Improvement

   b) Full House

   c) The Middle

   d) Modern Family

7. Which show, starring Kiefer Sutherland, follows the character Jack Bauer as he prevents terrorist attacks in real-time?

   a) 24

   b) Homeland

   c) The Shield

   d) Person of Interest

8. Which TV sitcom portrays the lives of two widowed people, each having three kids getting married and raising their families together?

   a) Twin Peaks

   b) Stranger Things

c) The Brady Bunch

d) The Haunting of Hill House

9. Which long-running TV show, created by Norman Lear, focuses on the lives of the Bunker family and deals with social issues of the time?

a) All in the Family

b) The Jeffersons

c) Maude

d) One Day at a Time

10. Which character from the HBO series Sex and the City dated a man who turns out to be an irredeemably bad kisser?

a) Miranda

b) Carrie

c) Samantha

d) Charlotte

11. Which high octane drama showcases the heroic everyday lives of firefighters, rescue squads and paramedics from Firehouse 51?

a) Chicago Fire

b) Emergency

c) As the World Turns

d) CHiPs

12. What drama series is based on two KGB spies in an arranged marriage who are posing as Americans in suburban Washington D.C.?

a) The Office

b) Knots Landing

c) The Americans

d) Scrubs

13. Which TV show, set in the 1980s, follows the lives of a group of friends in a small town dealing with supernatural events?

   a) Stranger Things

   b) The Goldbergs

   c) Freaks and Geeks

   d) The Dukes of Hazzard

14. Which TV show features a fictionalized version of the life of comedian Larry David, as he navigates everyday social interactions?

   a) Curb Your Enthusiasm

   b) Seinfeld

   c) Louis

   d) The Larry Sanders Show

15. Which TV show follows the lives of six friends living in New York City, with one of them being a paleontologist named _____?

   a) Mike Brady

   b) Andy Griffith

   c) Frank Costanza

   d) Ross Geller

16. Which show features a group of FBI agents investigating paranormal phenomena, with the lead character being Fox Mulder?

a) The X-Files

b) Fringe

c) Supernatural

d) Twin Peaks

17. Which TV sitcom focuses on a traditional suburban family with very liberal parents trying to raise an ambitious young conservative eldest son starring Michael J. Fox?

a) Roseanne

b) Married… with Children

c) The Simpsons

d) Family Ties

18. Which TV show follows the lives of the employees of a fictionalized news network, with characters like Aaron Sorkin's Will McAvoy?

a) The Newsroom

b) 30 Rock

c) Studio 60 on the Sunset Strip

d) West Wing

19. Which TV show, created by David Lynch, explores the murder of a high school girl in a small town with bizarre characters?

a) Twin Peaks

b) Fargo

c) The Killing

d) Broadchurch

20. The 90's sitcom Wings follows the lives of two brothers, Joe and Brian Hackett, who run a one-plane commuter service from a small airport located where?

   a) Martha's Vineyard

   b) Key West

   c) Long Island

   d) Nantucket

21. Which TV show involves a group of ambitious teens who try to escape the realities of high school by joining a glee club?

   a) Glee

   b) Riverdale

   c) Breaking Bad

   d) Happy Days

22. Who was the main character in the drama series based in North Jersey about an Italian American mobster?

   a) Tony Blundetto

   b) Silvio Dante

   c) Walter White

   d) Tony Soprano

23. Which TV series, known for its political drama, follows the personal and professional lives of President Jed Barlet's staff?

   a) The West Wing

   b) Veep

   c) House of Cards

   d) Designated Survivor

24. Which TV show, starring Jon Hamm, focuses on the lives of advertising executives in the 1960s?

   a) Mad Men

   b) Boardwalk Empire

   c) The Deuce

   d) The Americans

25. Which TV show, set in a dystopian future, revolves around a group of people fighting to survive in a world overrun by zombies?

   a) The Walking Dead

   b) The 100

   c) Battlestar Galactica

   d) Revolution

26. Which TV show, created by Tina Fey, takes place behind the scenes of a fictional live sketch comedy show?

   a) 30 Rock

   b) Parks and Recreation

   c) The Office

   d) Brooklyn Nine-Nine

27. Which TV sitcom features a family "moving on up to the East Side" starring Sherman Hemsley?

   a) All In the Family

   b) The Jeffersons

   c) Maude

d) The Love Boat

28. Which TV show features a doctor who uses unorthodox methods to diagnose patients with rare medical conditions?

   a) House

   b) ER

   c) Grey's Anatomy

   d) Private Practice

29. Which TV show, featuring a character named Lorelai Gilmore, revolves around the lives of a mother and daughter in a small Connecticut town?

   a) Gilmore Girls

   b) Parenthood

   c) The O.C.

   d) Dawson's Creek

30. Which TV series, created by Shonda Rhimes, follows the life of a defense attorney and her team of associates?

   a) How to Get Away with Murder

   b) Scandal

   c) Grey's Anatomy

   d) Private Practice

31. In the TV show, Cheers, Norm was married to a woman that was never seen on screen. What was her name?

   a) Diane

   b) Carla

c) Silvia

d) Vera

32. Which TV show, set in the world of high finance and featuring characters like Bobby Axelrod, explores corporate greed and power?

   a) Billions

   b) Succession

   c) Mad Men

   d) Industry

33. In season one of Friends, what was the name of Monica's love interest whom everyone loved and always seemed to be the life of the party, until he gave up drinking?

   a) Joey

   b) Ugly Naked Guy

   c) Fun Bobby

   d) Richard

34. What drama series focuses on introspective friends in a close-knit group based in Philadelphia featuring characters named Hope and Michael?

   a) Fantasy Island

   b) ER

   c) Eight is Enough

   d) Thirtysomething

35. In the series Sanford and Son, Fred often fakes having a certain medical condition to gain sympathy. What was his fake ailment?

   a) Heat Attack

b) Blindness

c) Deafness

d) Sprained ankle

36. Which TV show, featuring a group of teenagers in a fictional high school, deals with themes of adolescence and supernatural elements based on a 1992 comedy movie?

   a) Buffy the Vampire Slayer

   b) The Vampire Diaries

   c) Stranger Things

   d) Riverdale

37. Before finding fame as Walter White on Breaking Bad, Bryan Cranston often appeared on the sitcom Seinfeld as a dentist. What was his name?

   a) Jay Peterman

   b) Cosmo Kramer

   c) Jake Jarmel

   d) Tim Whatley

38. Which TV series features a detective solving crimes in a futuristic city with a focus on high-tech gadgets and artificial intelligence?

   a) Minority Report

   b) Person of Interest

   c) Altered Carbon

   d) Blade Runner: Black Lotus

39. Which TV show focuses on the personal and professional lives of a group of surgeons working at a prestigious hospital in Seattle?

a) Grey's Anatomy

b) ER

c) House

d) Private Practice

40. One of the actors from the 80's hit drama Hill Street Blues also played in the NFL for the Minnesota Vikings and for Cornell University Big Red. Name the actor.

a) Taurean Blacque

b) Daniel J. Travanti

c) Dennis Franz

d) Ed Marinaro

41. In the cartoon SpongeBob SquarePants, what is Mr. Krab's daughter's name?

a) Starfish Krabs

b) Pearl Krabs

c) Sundance Krabs

d) Valerie Krabs

42. Which TV show features a character named Walter White, who turns to manufacturing methamphetamine after a terminal cancer diagnosis?

a) Breaking Bad

b) Sons of Anarchy

c) Narcos

d) Better Call Saul

43. Which TV series, set in the world of professional wrestling, follows the lives of wrestlers both inside and outside the ring?

a) Glow

b) Heels

c) Wrestling with Shadows

d) Dark Side of the Ring

44. Which TV show, set in the world of a high-tech startup, revolves around the lives of eccentric tech developers and their personal relationships?

a) Silicon Valley

b) Halt and Catch Fire

c) Devs

d) The IT Crowd

45. Which TV show, starring Amy Poehler, features the lives of employees in the Parks Department of a fictional small town?

a) Parks and Recreation

b) The Office

c) Community

d) Brooklyn Nine-Nine

46. Which 1970's TV sitcom, featuring characters like Lenny and Squiggy, is set in Milwaukee?

a) Lavern & Shirley

b) Shotz Brewery

c) Happy Days

d) Columbo

47. Which TV series, set in the 1950s, follows the lives of a group of aspiring actresses trying to make it in Hollywood?

   a) Hollywood

   b) Feud

   c) The Marvelous Mrs. Maisel

   d) Mad Men

48. Which late 1990's TV show, starring Ryan Reynolds, focuses on two twenty-somethings living in Boston above a pizza place?

   a) Breaking Bad

   b) The Days and Nights of Molly Dodd

   c) The Simple Life

   d) Two Guys and a Girl

49. Which TV show, set in a fictional high school, features a group of students with superpowers and their adventures?

   a) Heroes

   b) The Secret Circle

   c) The Vampire Diaries

   d) Riverdale

50. Which TV show, featuring a diverse cast of characters working at a paper company, is known for its mockumentary style?

   a) The Office

   b) Parks and Recreation

   c) Modern Family

   d) Brooklyn Nine-Nine

Answers:

1. d) Ozark

2. b) Outer Banks

3. d) Charlie's Angels

4. b) Scandal

5. a) The Big Bang Theory

6. a) Home Improvement

7. a) 24

8. c) The Brady Bunch

9. a) All in the Family

10. d) Charlotte

11. a) Chicago Fire

12. c) The Americans

13. a) Stranger Things

14. a) Curb Your Enthusiasm

15. d) Ross Geller

16. a) The X-Files

17. d) Family Ties

18. a) The Newsroom

19. a) Twin Peaks

20. d) Nantucket

21. a) Glee

22. d) Tony Soprano

23. a) The West Wing

24. a) Mad Men

25. a) The Walking Dead

26. a) 30 Rock

27. b) The Jeffersons

28. a) House

29. a) Gilmore Girls

30. a) How to Get Away with Murder

31. d) Vera

32. a) Billions

33. c) Fun Bobby

34. d) Thirtysomething

35. a) Heart Attack

36. a) Buffy the Vampire Slayer

37. d) Tim Whatley

38. b) Person of Interest

39. a) Grey's Anatomy

40. a) The Goldbergs

41. b) Pearl Krabs

42. a) Breaking Bad

43. a) Glow

44. a) Silicon Valley

45. a) Parks and Recreation

46. a) Lavern & Shirley

47. c) The Marvelous Mrs. Maisel

48. d) Two Guys and a Girl

49. a) Heroes

50. a) The Office

Chapter 13

America's National Parks, Rivers & Lakes

1. The Grand Canyon is in which state?

   a) Arizona

   b) Utah

   c) Colorado

   d) Nevada

2. Yosemite National Park is renowned for its stunning granite cliffs and waterfalls, and it is situated in which state?

   a) California

   b) Oregon

   c) Washington

   d) Nevada

3. The Mississippi River flows into which large body of water?

   a) Great Lakes

   b) Atlantic Ocean

   c) Gulf of Mexico

   d) Pacific Ocean

4. Denali National Park is home to the highest peak in North America. In which state is it located?

   a) Alaska

   b) Washington

   c) Oregon

   d) Montana

5. The Great Salt Lake is known for its high salinity and is found in which state?

a) Utah

b) Colorado

c) Nevada

d) Arizona

6. Yellowstone National Park spans parts of which three states?

    a) Wyoming, Montana, and Idaho

    b) Utah, Colorado, and New Mexico

    c) Washington, Oregon, and California

    d) Alaska, Washington, and Oregon

7. The Colorado River is famous for carving out which major landmark?

    a) Grand Canyon

    b) Yellowstone Falls

    c) Niagara Falls

    d) Great Smoky Mountains

8. The largest man-made lake in the United States besides the Great Lakes?

    a) Lake Superior

    b) Lake Oahe

    c) Long Lake

    d) Lake Erie

9. The Everglades National Park is in which state?

    a) Florida

    b) Texas

c) Louisiana

d) Georgia

10. Mount Rushmore is in which National Park?

   a) Badlands National Park

   b) Theodore Roosevelt National Park

   c) Custer State Park

   d) Mount Rushmore National Memorial

11. The Columbia River flows through several states, including which two?

   a) Oregon and Washington

   b) California and Nevada

   c) North Carolina and South Carolina

   d) Utah and Colorado

12. The most visited National Park in the United States is

   a) Zion National Park

   b) Yellowstone National Park

   c) Yosemite National Park

   d) Great Smoky Mountains National Park

13. Glacier National Park is in which state, known for its stunning glaciers and rugged terrain?

   a) Montana

   b) Idaho

   c) Wyoming

d) Colorado

14. The famous natural landmark, Old Faithful, is in which National Park?

   a) Yellowstone National Park

   b) Grand Canyon National Park

   c) Zion National Park

   d) Yosemite National Park

15. The largest national park in the contiguous United States is.

   a) Rocky Mountain National Park

   b) Grand Canyon National Park

   c) Great Smoky Mountains National Park

   d) Death Valley National Park

16. The Rio Grande River forms part of the border between which two countries?

   a) United States and Mexico

   b) Canada and United States

   c) United States and Canada

   d) United States and Guatemala

17. The famous rock formation, El Capitan, is found in which National Park?

   a) Yosemite National Park

   b) Zion National Park

   c) Grand Canyon National Park

   d) Rocky Mountain National Park

18. The Missouri River is the longest river in the United States. It flows through how many states?

   a) 10

   b) 8

   c) 7

   d) 12

19. Which lake is known for its crystal-clear blue water and is a popular destination in Montana?

   a) Lake Tahoe

   b) Flathead Lake

   c) Crater Lake

   d) Lake Michigan

20. The tallest waterfall in the United States, Yosemite Falls, is in which National Park?

   a) Yosemite National Park

   b) Grand Canyon National Park

   c) Olympic National Park

   d) Glacier National Park

21. Which national park has one of the densest populations of black bears documented with the United States?

   a) Shenandoah National Park

   b) Great Smoky Mountains National Park

   c) Blue Ridge Parkway

   d) Cuyahoga Valley National Park

22. Which national park is home to Kolob Arch, one of the largest and longest natural arches in the world?

   a) Arches National Park

   b) Bryce Canyon National Park

   c) Zion National Park

   d) Canyonlands National Park

23. The iconic geysers and hot springs of the geothermal area are in which National Park?

   a) Yellowstone National Park

   b) Lassen Volcanic National Park

   c) Glacier National Park

   d) Crater Lake National Park

24. Which picturesque Adirondack Mountain town played host to the 1980 Winter Olympic Games?

   a) Saranac Lake

   b) Lake Placid

   c) Old Forge

   d) Plattsburgh

25. The scenic Blue Ridge Parkway stretches through which two states?

   a) North Carolina and Virginia

   b) South Carolina and Georgia

   c) Tennessee and Kentucky

   d) West Virginia and Maryland

26. A critically acclaimed black and white photograph was taken by Ansel Adams in 1942 of which mountain range?

a) Adirondack Mountains

b) Grand Teton Mountains

c) Sierra Nevada

d) Cascade Range

27. The smallest freshwater lake by volume in the United States is.

a) Lake Superior

b) Lake Michigan

c) Lake Huron

d) Lake Erie

28. The iconic monument, Mount Rushmore, features the faces of four American presidents: George Washington, Thomas Jefferson, Abraham Lincoln and _____.

a) James Madison

b) Franklin D. Roosevelt

c) Harry S. Truman

d) Theodore Roosevelt

29. The famous geological formation, the Hoodoos, can be found in which National Park known for its unique rock formations?

a) Bryce Canyon National Park

b) Arches National Park

c) Canyonlands National Park

d) Zion National Park

30. The Everglades National Park is home to which unique type of ecosystem?

   a) Desert

   b) Wetlands

   c) Alpine

   d) Forest

31. The Yellowstone River flows through which National Park and is known for its spectacular waterfalls?

   a) Yellowstone National Park

   b) Grand Canyon National Park

   c) Rocky Mountain National Park

   d) Yosemite National Park

32. The picturesque Crater Lake, known for its deep blue color, is in which state?

   a) Idaho

   b) California

   c) Washington

   d) Oregon

33. The scenic Hoh Rain Forest is located within which National Park known for its lush vegetation?

   a) Olympic National Park

   b) Great Smoky Mountains National Park

   c) Shenandoah National Park

   d) Redwood National Park

34. The famous National Park, known for its ancient redwood trees, is called

a) Redwood National and State Parks

b) Yosemite National Park

c) Sequoia National Park

d) Joshua Tree National Park

35. The Mississippi River is one of the longest rivers in the United States, flowing through which central city?

a) St. Louis, Missouri

b) New Orleans

c) Memphis

d) All of the above

36. The majestic Half Dome is a well-known rock formation in which National Park?

a) Yosemite National Park

b) Zion National Park

c) Grand Canyon National Park

d) Glacier National Park

37. The picturesque Badlands National Park is in which state?

a) South Dakota

b) North Dakota

c) Montana

d) Nebraska

38. The Colorado River flows through seven US states, including Arizona, Colorado, Nevada, New Mexico, Utah, Wyoming and _____?

a) Nebraska

b) Texas

c) California

d) Montana

39. The iconic rock formation known as Delicate Arch is found in which National Park?

a) Arches National Park

b) Bryce Canyon National Park

c) Zion National Park

d) Capitol Reef National Park

40. The Chattahoochee River flows through which southeastern state known for its Southern charm?

a) North Carolina

b) Florida

c) Georgia

d) South Carolina

41. The majestic glacier-carved scenery of Glacier Bay is in which state?

a) Alaska

b) Washington

c) Oregon

d) California

42. The scenic park featuring colorful rock formations and canyons, known as Canyonlands, is in which state?

a) Kansas

b) Utah

c) Arizona

d) New Mexico

43. The Great Lakes consists of five lakes. Which one is the largest by surface area?

    a) Lake Superior

    b) Lake Michigan

    c) Lake Huron

    d) Lake Erie

44. The famous National Park known for its stunning mountain vistas and rich wildlife, known as Rocky Mountain, is in which state?

    a) Oklahoma

    b) Wyoming

    c) Colorado

    d) Utah

45. The Potomac River flows through which iconic American city?

    a) Boston

    b) Philadelphia

    c) New York City

    d) Washington, D.C.

46. The serene and scenic lake known for its picturesque beauty and outdoor recreation, named Lake Tahoe, straddles the border of which two states?

    a) California and Nevada

    b) Oregon and Washington

    c) Colorado and Utah

d) Arizona and New Mexico

47. The National Park known for its ancient Native American cliff dwellings, Mesa Verde, is in which state?

   a) Colorado

   b) New Mexico

   c) Utah

   d) Arizona

48. The famous National Park known for its deep canyons and rock spires, Bryce Canyon, is in which state?

   a) Arizona

   b) Utah

   c) Colorado

   d) Nevada

49. The stunning and vast expanse of Death Valley National Park is in which state?

   a) California

   b) Nevada

   c) Arizona

   d) Utah

50. Name the large river that flows through several states in the Mid-Atlantic region of America, providing water to millions. It is the longest free-flowing river in the Eastern United States. (Hint- George Washington)

   a) Hudson River

   b) Connecticut River

c) Delaware River

d) Allegheny River

Answers:

1. a) Arizona

2. a) California

3. c) Gulf of Mexico

4. a) Alaska

5. a) Utah

6. a) Wyoming, Montana, and Idaho

7. a) Grand Canyon

8. b) Lake Oahe

9. a) Florida

10. d) Mount Rushmore National Memorial

11. a) Oregon and Washington

12. d) Great Smoky Mountains National Park

13. a) Montana

14. a) Yellowstone National Park

15. d) Death Valley National Park

16. a) United States and Mexico

17. a) Yosemite National Park

18. c) 7

19. b) Flathead Lake

20. a) Yosemite National Park

21. a) Shenandoah National Park

22. c) Zion National Park

23. a) Yellowstone National Park

24. b) Lake Placid

25. a) North Carolina and Virginia

26. b) Grand Tetons

27. d) Lake Erie

28. d) Theodore Roosevelt

29. a) Bryce Canyon National Park

30. b) Wetlands

31. a) Yellowstone National Park

32. d) Oregon

33. a) Olympic National Park

34. a) Redwood National and State Parks

35. a) St. Louis, Missouri

36. a) Yosemite National Park

37. a) South Dakota

38. c) California

39. a) Arches National Park

40. c) Georgia

41. a) Alaska

42. b) Utah

43. a) Lake Superior

44. c) Colorado

45. d) Washington, D.C.

46. a) California and Nevada

47. a) Colorado

48. b) Utah

49. a) California

50. c) Delaware River

Chapter 14

America's Mountains and Mountain Ranges

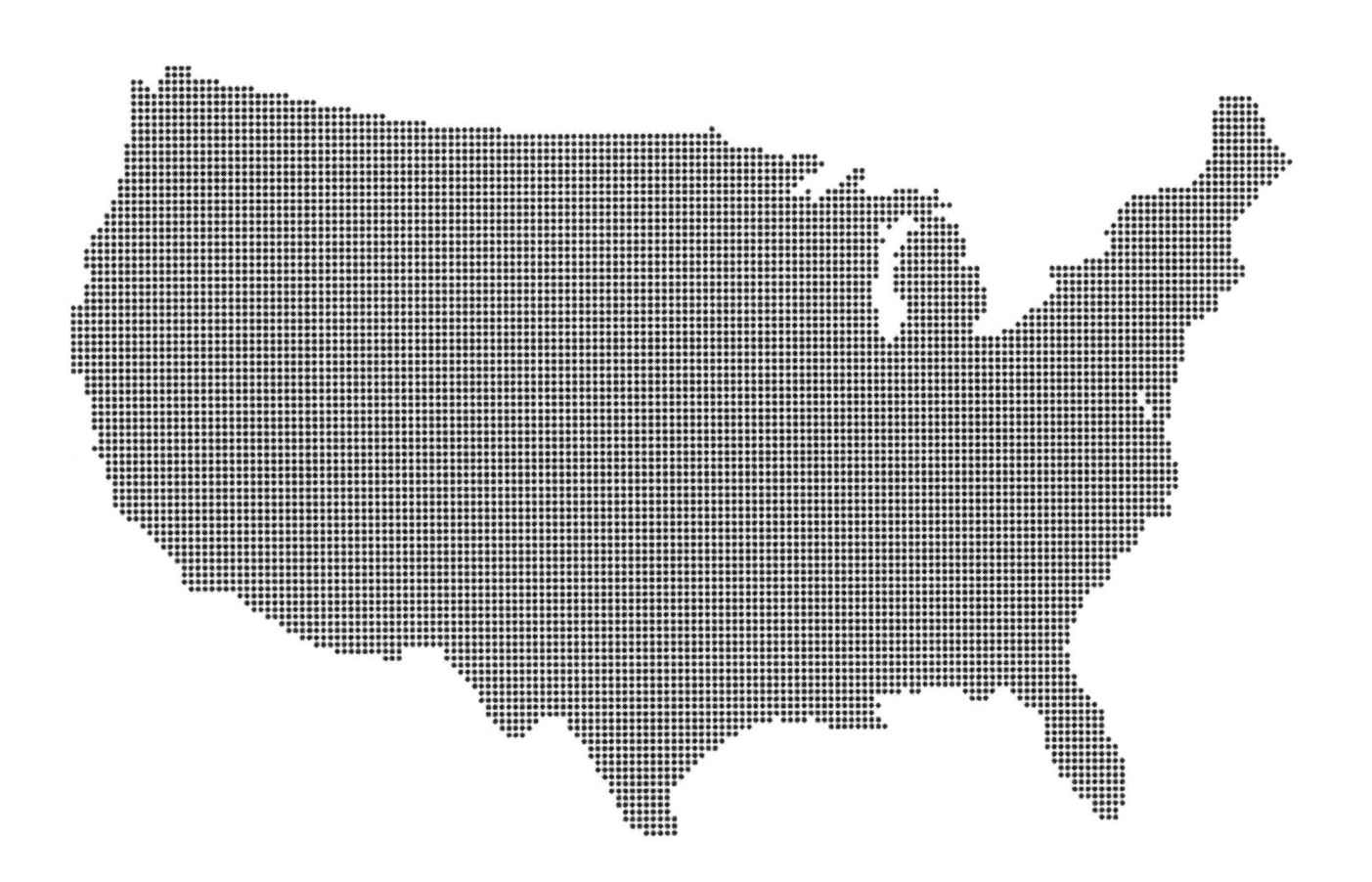

1. Mount Everest is the highest peak in the world, but what is the highest peak in the United States? This peak had an official name change in 2016 to "Denali".

   a) Mount McKinley

   b) Mount Whitney

   c) Mount Rainier

   d) Mount Hood

2. The Rocky Mountains extend from the United States into which country?

   a) Nova Scotia

   b) Mexico

   c) Canada

   d) Honduras

3. What is the name of the mountain range that runs along the eastern United States?

   a) Appalachian Mountains

   b) Sierra Nevada

   c) Cascade Range

   d) Rocky Mountains

4. Mount Whitney is the tallest peak in the contiguous United States. In which state is it located?

   a) California

   b) Nevada

   c) Colorado

   d) Utah

5. The Cascade Range is known for its volcanic activity. Which of the following volcanoes is in this range?

   a) Mount St. Helens

   b) Mount Hood

   c) Mount Rainier

   d) All of the above

6. The Sierra Nevada Mountains are in which two states?

   a) California and Nevada

   b) Oregon and Washington

   c) Colorado and New Mexico

   d) Utah and Idaho

7. Which mountain range separates the eastern United States from the central plains?

   a) Appalachian Mountains

   b) Rocky Mountains

   c) Sierra Nevada

   d) Cascades

8. The Great Smoky Mountains are part of which larger mountain range?

   a) Appalachian Mountains

   b) Rocky Mountains

   c) Sierra Nevada

   d) Cascades

9. The Grand Teton Mountain range is in which U.S. state?

a) Montana

b) Wyoming

c) Colorado

d) Utah

10. Mount Rushmore, famous for its presidential carvings, is in which mountain range?

   a) Black Hills

   b) Sierra Nevada

   c) Rocky Mountains

   d) Appalachian Mountains

11. Which mountain is the most prominent summit in the entire Appalachian Mountains?

   a) Mount Marcy

   b) Mount Washington

   c) Pikes Peak

   d) Mount Mitchell

12. The Appalachian Trail stretches from Georgia to Maine. What mountain range does it primarily traverse?

   a) Appalachian Mountains

   b) Sierra Nevada

   c) Rocky Mountains

   d) Cascades

13. The highest peak in the Sierra Nevada range is

   a) Mount Whitney

b) Mount Hood

c) Mount Rainier

d) Mount Shasta

14. The Rockies are known for their stunning beauty and vast wilderness. Which U.S. national park is part of this mountain range?

    a) Rocky Mountain National Park

    b) Zion National Park

    c) Yellowstone National Park

    d) Yosemite National Park

15. The Bitterroot Range is in which two states?

    a) Montana and Idaho

    b) Washington and Oregon

    c) Wyoming and Colorado

    d) California and Nevada

16. Which of the following is NOT a peak in the Cascade Range?

    a) Mount Rainier

    b) Mount Hood

    c) Mount Shasta

    d) Mount McKinley

17. Crayola named a crayon for this Colorado mountain in the shade of purple in 2004.

    a) Mount Blue Sky

    b) Mount Elbert

c) Longs Peak

d) Pikes Peak

18. Which mountain range extends into parts of Mexico and is known for its high peaks and dramatic scenery?

   a) Sierra Nevada

   b) Rocky Mountains

   c) Sierra Madre

   d) Cascade Range

19. Which famous U.S. peak is known for its unique dome shape and is a popular climbing destination?

   a) El Capitan

   b) Half Dome

   c) Mount Hood

   d) Mount St. Helens

20. The San Juan Mountains are in which state?

   a) Colorado

   b) Utah

   c) Nevada

   d) New Mexico

21. The Wasatch Range is part of which state's mountain system?

   a) Idaho

   b) Colorado

   c) Wyoming

d) Utah

22. The Teton Range is known for its rugged peaks and stunning scenery. What is the tallest peak in this range?

   a) Grand Teton

   b) Middle Teton

   c) South Teton

   d) Mount Moran

23. The Adirondack Mountains are in which state?

   a) Maine

   b) New Hampshire

   c) New York

   d) Massachusetts

24. The Great Basin is characterized by its unique geography. What mountain range forms the eastern boundary of this basin?

   a) Wasatch Range

   b) Sierra Nevada

   c) Rocky Mountains

   d) Cascade Range

25. Mount Elbert is the highest peak in which mountain range?

   a) Adirondack Mountains

   b) Sierra Nevada

   c) Cascade Range

   d) Sawatch Range

26. The Green Mountains are a prominent feature of which northeastern state?

    a) Vermont

    b) Maine

    c) New Hampshire

    d) Massachusetts

27. The Uinta Mountains are unique for their east-west orientation. In which state are they primarily located?

    a) Colorado

    b) Utah

    c) Wyoming

    d) Montana

28. Which of the following mountain ranges is known for its dramatic spires and deep canyons, particularly in Utah?

    a) Wasatch Range

    b) San Juan Mountains

    c) Colorado Plateau

    d) Uinta Mountains

29. The Adirondack Mountains in New York have 46 High Peaks. Which is the highest peak?

    a) Mount Haystack

    b) Mount Marcy

    c) Mount Skylight

    d) Upper Wolfjaw Mountain

30. Which U.S. state is home to the volcanic peak Mount Shasta?

   a) California

   b) Oregon

   c) Washington

   d) Nevada

31. The Rocky Mountains stretch from Canada to the southern United States. What is the highest peak in the Colorado Rockies?

   a) Mount Harvard

   b) Mount Massive

   c) Longs Peak

   d) Mount Elbert

32. The highest peak in the U.S. state of Washington is.

   a) Mount Rainier

   b) Mount Hood

   c) Mount Baker

   d) Mount St. Helens

33. The Smoky Mountains are renowned for their misty appearance and are part of which U.S. National Park?

   a) Great Smoky Mountains National Park

   b) Shenandoah National Park

   c) Yellowstone National Park

   d) Zion National Park

34. Mount Hood is a prominent peak in which mountain range?

a) Cascade Range

b) Sierra Nevada

c) Rocky Mountains

d) Adirondack Mountains

35. The Black Hills are known for their historical significance and unique rock formations. In which state are they located?

a) North Dakota

b) South Dakota

c) Montana

d) Wyoming

36. The Sierra Nevada range includes which famous national park known for its giant sequoia trees?

a) Sequoia National Park

b) Yosemite National Park

c) Kings Canyon National Park

d) Zion National Park

37. The White Mountains are a prominent feature of which northeastern state?

a) New Hampshire

b) Maine

c) Vermont

d) Massachusetts

38. The highest wind gust ever recorded at 231 miles per hour in 1934 occurred on what mountain which is known for its extreme weather? (Hint: New England)

a) Mount Sanford

b) Mount Foraker

c) Mount Washington

d) Mount Marcy

39. The second highest peak in the Adirondack Mountains?

   a) Grand Teton

   b) Algonquin Peak

   c) Mount Colden

   d) Basin Mountain

40. The San Gabriel Mountains are a prominent feature in which state?

   a) California

   b) Arizona

   c) Nevada

   d) Utah

41. Which mountain range is known for its extensive system of caves, including Mammoth Cave?

   a) Appalachian Mountains

   b) Rocky Mountains

   c) Sierra Nevada

   d) Ozark Mountains

42. The most photographed mountains in the U.S. are two bell-shaped peaks, Maroon Peak and North Maroon Peak, also known as The Maroon Bells. They are buried deep in the

Rocky Mountains within the White River National Forest between Crested Butte, Colorado and another famous ski town.

   a) Telluride

   b) Aspen

   c) Beaver Creek

   d) Steamboat

43. The Southern Appalachian Mountains are home to which national park known for its biodiversity? This national park is considered to have the highest level of biological diversity within the entire US National Park system.

   a) Great Smoky Mountains National Park

   b) Shenandoah National Park

   c) Cuyahoga Valley National Park

   d) Mammoth Cave National Park

44. The Cascade Range extends into which Canadian province?

   a) British Columbia

   b) Alberta

   c) Manitoba

   d) Ontario

45. The St. Elias Mountains are in which U.S. state?

   a) Oregan

   b) Washington

   c) Alaska

   d) Idaho

46. The Klamath Mountains are in which two states?

   a) California and Oregon

   b) Washington and Idaho

   c) Nevada and Utah

   d) Montana and Wyoming

47. The Blue Ridge Mountains are a part of which larger mountain range?

   a) Appalachian Mountains

   b) Rocky Mountains

   c) Sierra Nevada

   d) Cascade Range

48. This mountain range is the northernmost extension of the Rocky Mountains in northern Alaska and is the only mountain range in the U.S. that one can view the Arctic Ocean from.

   a) Brooks Range

   b) Denali

   c) Mount Saint Elias

   d) Mount Silverthrone

49. Which mountain range features the highest peak in the state of New Mexico?

   a) Sangre de Cristo Mountains

   b) Sandia Mountains

   c) Jemez Mountains

   d) Organ Mountains

50. The movies "The Eiger Sanction", "Butch Cassidy and the Sundance Kid", "Romancing the Stone", and "Jeremiah Johnson" were film in the National Park?

a) Grand Teton

b) Badlands

c) Acadia

d) Zion

Answers:

1. a) Mount McKinley

2. c) Canada

3. a) Appalachian Mountains

4. a) California

5. d) All of the above

6. a) California and Nevada

7. a) Appalachian Mountains

8. a) Appalachian Mountains

9. b) Wyoming

10. a) Black Hills

11. d) Mount Mitchell

12. a) Appalachian Mountains

13. a) Mount Whitney

14. a) Rocky Mountain National Park

15. a) Montana and Idaho

16. d) Mount McKinley

17. d) Pikes Peak

18. c) Sierra Madre

19. b) Half Dome

20. a) Colorado

21. d) Utah

22. a) Grand Teton

23. c) New York

24. a) Wasatch Range

25. d) Sawatch Range

26. a) Vermont

27. b) Utah

28. d) Uinta Mountains

29. b) Mount Marcy

30. a) California

31. d) Mount Elbert

32. a) Mount Rainier

33. a) Great Smoky Mountains National Park

34. a) Cascade Range

35. b) South Dakota

36. a) Sequoia National Park

37. a) New Hampshire

38. c) Mount Washington

39. b) Algonquin Peak

40. a) California

41. a) Appalachian Mountains

42. b) Aspen

43. a) Great Smoky Mountains National Park

44. a) British Columbia

45. c) Alaska

46. a) California and Oregon

47. a) Appalachian Mountains

48. a) Brooks Range

49. a) Sangre de Cristo Mountains

50. d) Zion

Thank you for your purchase

Please leave a review if you enjoyed this trivia book!

Made in United States
Orlando, FL
26 March 2025